Welcome to *Texas Write Source*!

This *Texas Write Source* book was written just for you. We hope you have fun and learn, too.

Enjoy writing!

Using Your *Texas Write Source* Book

Your *Texas Write Source* book includes lessons and tips about writing. You will learn to write letters, reports, stories, poems, and more.

You will learn how to wri and speak in class. Finally, a section called the "Proofreade explains the rules of writing.

TEXAS WRITE SOURCE

Authors
Dave Kemper, Patrick Sebranek, and Verne Meyer

Consulting Author
Gretchen Bernabei

Illustrator
Chris Krenzke

GREAT SOURCE®

HOUGHTON MIFFLIN HARCOURT

www.hmheducation.com/tx/writesource

Trademarks and trade names are shown in this book strictly for illustrative purposes and are the property of their respective owners. The authors' references herein should not be regarded as affecting their validity.

Printed in the U.S.A.

ISBN-13   978-0-547-39471-8

2 3 4 5 6 7 8 9 10 0914 19 18 17 16 15 14 13 12 11

4500305565   B C D E F G

Quick Guide

Contents

Texas Write Source

The Writing Process

The Forms of Writing

Descriptive Writing

Narrative Writing

Expository Writing

Persuasive Writing

Response to Texts

Creative Writing

Report Writing

The Tools of Language

Basic Grammar and Writing

A Writer's Resource

Proofreader's Guide

Why Write?

The main reason to write is to communicate with others. Writing is an important way to share your feelings, thoughts, stories, and ideas.

Writing will help you . . .

- **Share with others.** You can tell your friends and family all about you in letters, cards, notes, and e-mail messages.

- **Remember more.** You can remember better when you write facts and ideas in your own words.

- **Learn more about you.** You will discover your own thoughts and feelings by writing.

- **Have fun.** You can imagine wonderful things in the stories, poems, and plays you write.

Remember: **The more you read, the better your writing will be.**

ELPS 1A, 2C, 3E, 3G, 4G

The Writing Process

Writing Focus

- Using the Writing Process
- Understanding the Texas Traits of Writing
- Evaluating Your Writing

Learning Language

Work with a partner. Read the meanings and share answers to the questions.

1. A draft is a piece of writing that you have not finished yet.
   Why might you write a draft first?
2. A process is an order of steps.
   Tell the process of making a sandwich.
3. When you talk it over, you share ideas.
   Which kind of pet is best? Talk it over with a partner.

Writers do their work in many different ways. Tim slowly builds his stories, thinking carefully about each new idea. Gina finds it helpful to draw pictures as she writes. José likes to talk about his writing as he goes along. There are many ways to get ready to write.

In this part of the book, you will learn all about writing from using the writing process to publishing your writing.

ELPS 3E, 3G

Using the
Writing Process

Do you have stories to tell, reports to give, letters to send, invitations to write, and ideas to share? Well then, join us in learning about the writing process and see what you can create.

Talk it over.

1. What is your favorite piece of writing?
2. How did you write it?

Prewriting ▶ Planning Your Writing

When you prewrite, you **choose** your topic and **gather** details about it.

Drafting ▶ Writing the First Draft

When you write a first draft, you **identify** your topic and **add** supporting details.

Revising ▶ Improving Your Writing

When you revise, you **change** parts to make your writing better. **Use** the traits of writing as a guide.

Editing ▶ Checking for Conventions

When you edit, you **check** for grammar, spelling, punctuation, and capitalization errors. Then you **correct** any that you find.

Publishing ▶ Sharing Your Final Copy

When you publish your writing, you **make** a neat, final copy and **share** it with others.

6

One Writer's Process

Monica's class had fun learning about holidays from around the world. Monica's teacher asked each student to write a paragraph about one of the holidays.

Follow along to see how Monica used the steps in the writing process to complete her paragraph.

Prewriting ▶ Planning Your Writing

When you prewrite, you choose your topic and gather details about it. You can use drawings during prewriting.

Choose Monica decided to write about a special holiday in Japan, Children's Day.

Study Monica remembered what she had learned about her topic in class. She also read about her topic.

Draw Monica drew pictures of the details she wanted to write about.

Monica's Pictures

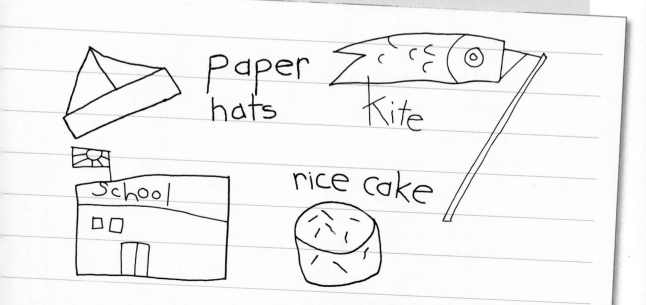

 **TEKS** 2.17B
ELPS 2C

Drafting ▶ Writing the First Draft

When you write your first draft, you put your ideas in sentence form.

> These are the things Monica did to write her first draft.
>
> **Look**   Before she started writing, Monica looked at her drawings about Children's Day.
>
> **State**   In her first sentence, Monica told what she would write about.
>
> **Add**   Monica's next sentences added ideas and details about her topic.

Most of the details in my paragraph come from my pictures.

Monica's First Draft

I lerned about Children's Day in school. It is a special day for kids in Japan. They do fun stuff on this day. It comes on May 5. Children do not go to school on Children's Day they fly colorful fish kites from tall poles. They where paper hats and eat rice cakes. i think the fish kites would be fun to see. I wonder if rice cakes taste good.

Talk it over.

Which details from her pictures (page 7) did Monica include in her first draft?

 **TEKS** 2.17C
ELPS 2C

Revising ▶ Improving Your Writing

When you revise, you try to improve your writing. You should change any parts that are unclear or hard to follow.

This is what Monica did to revise her paragraph.

Review   Monica read her first draft to herself.

Share   Next, Monica shared her first draft with a classmate.

Improve   Then she changed parts to improve her writing.

I moved one idea and replaced another one. I also added a new detail.

Monica's Revising

I lerned about Children's Day in school. It is a special day for kids in Japan. ~~They do fun stuff~~ Children have fun on this day. It comes on May 5. Children do not go to school on Children's Day they fly colorful fish kites from tall poles. They where paper hats and eat rice cakes wrapped in leaves. i think the fish kites would be fun to see. I wonder if rice cakes taste good.

Talk it over.

What changes did Monica make?

TEKS 2.17D
ELPS 2C

Editing ▶ Checking for Conventions

When you edit, you check for correct grammar, spelling, punctuation, and capitalization.

This is what Monica did to edit her writing.

Read   Monica read her revised paragraph for conventions.

Correct   Monica used the rubric on page 30. Then she corrected any grammar, capitalization, punctuation, and spelling mistakes she found.

Recheck   Monica checked her writing one last time for mistakes.

I used the editing marks listed on page 451. I also added a title—Children's Day!

Monica's Editing

Children's Day

I ~~lerned~~ *learned* about Children's Day

in school. It comes on May 5. It

is a special day for kids in Japan.

Children have fun on this day.

Children do not go to school on

Children's Day ⊙ T they fly colorful fish

kites from tall poles. They ~~where~~ *wear*

paper hats and eat rice cakes

wrapped in leaves. i think the fish

kites would be fun to see. I wonder

if rice cakes taste good.

Talk it over.

Which convention errors did Monica correct?

TEKS 2.17E
ELPS 2C

Publishing ▶ **Sharing Your Writing**

When you publish your writing, you make a final copy and share it with others.

This is what Monica did to publish her writing.

Complete   Monica made a final copy of her paragraph. She skipped a line after her title and indented the first line of her paragraph. Monica included all of her changes and corrections. She used good handwriting.

Share   Then Monica shared her paragraph by reading it out loud to her classmates.

I decided to draw a fish kite on my final copy.

Monica's Paragraph

Children's Day

▶ (Skip)

▶ (Indent) I learned about Children's Day in school. It comes on May 5. It is a special day for kids in Japan. Children have fun on this day. Children do not go to school on Children's Day. They fly colorful fish kites from tall poles. They wear paper hats and eat rice cakes wrapped in leaves. I think the fish kites would be fun to see. I wonder if rice cakes taste good.

Talk it over.

1. What details in Monica's paragraph do you like the best? Name two.
2. What thoughts does Monica share in the last two sentences?

Working with a
Partner

In art class, Luis made a coil pot, and he decided to write a story about it. He shared his story with a partner. She asked some questions and that gave Luis some good ideas to make his story even better.

Helping One Another

Being a partner and having a partner is helpful as you go through the writing process. Here are some ways partners can help one another.

Talk   Partners can talk about topics and details. Talking can help you **prewrite** and draft.

Listen and Ask   Partners can listen while a first draft is shared out loud. Partners ask questions to help **revise** the writing.

Check   Partners can help check writing for conventions. Working together can help edit the writing.

Read   Partners can read and enjoy a final copy. Reading is one way to **publish**.

Learning Language

Partners are two people who help each other. How can a **partner** help you write? Talk about it with a **partner**.

TEKS 2.17E
ELPS 2D, 2I, 3E

Being on a Team

Working with a partner is like being on a team. After writing a first draft, one team member reads his or her writing out loud. The other member listens and responds to the writing.

Partner ips

When You Are the Writer

Tell why you chose your topic.
Read your writing to your partner.
Pay attention to your partner's comments.

When You Are the Listener

Look at your partner.
Listen carefully to the writing.
Respond to the writing.
  1. **Tell** your partner what you like.
  2. **Ask** any questions you may have.

Using a Response Sheet

You can also use a response sheet to review your partner's writing.

Laura's Response

Response Sheet

Writer: <u>Luis</u>   Listener: <u>Laura</u>

Title: <u>My Coil Pot</u>

1. One thing I like about your story:

   <u>I like the way you told about</u>

   <u>making the long snake of clay.</u>

2. One question I have about your story:

   <u>Who are you going to give the</u>

   <u>pot to?</u>

Understanding the
Texas Traits of Writing

You can use the **Texas traits of writing** listed below to help you do your best writing.

Focus — Write about one main idea.

Organization — Make your writing easy to follow.

Development of Ideas — Use details to develop your topic.

Voice — Sound like you are really interested in your topic.

Conventions — Follow the rules for writing.

Focus

Write about one main idea.

Carlos wrote about his new friend. All of his details are about that topic.

My New Friend

My best friend Steve moved away. He lived next door. I was sad to see him go. Who would move into Steve's house?

One morning, a big moving van came to Steve's house. A boy sat on the front steps, looking sad. His name was Mario.

Mario told me that he was lonely because he missed his old friends. I asked Mario to play soccer with me. Now we both have a new friend.

 TEKS 2.17B, 2.18A, 2.21A(vii)

Organization — Make your writing easy to follow.

Cole makes sure that his writing is easy to follow from beginning to end.

Our Sailing Adventure

The Beginning names the topic.

Last summer, I had an adventure with my grandma. We went sailing on a tall ship in the harbor in Baltimore.

The Middle adds details. The words in blue show order.

First, we pulled on ropes to help put up the sails. Then we sailed out to sea. Soon we couldn't even see land. Squawking seagulls flew around us. When the crew first fired a cannon, the noise and smoke scared me. Then I started laughing.

The Ending shares my final thought.

Grandma and I had a great time. I can't wait for our next adventure.

Development of Ideas

Use details to develop your topic.

Anita thinks of details about her baby sister and adds the details to a cluster. Then she uses the cluster to write.

looks like me

three months old

sleeps a lot

my baby sister

cries when she is hungry

smiles at me

wears pink and yellow

practice

1. Make your own cluster. Write your topic in the center. Add at least four details around it.
2. Share your ideas with a partner.

Voice **Sound like you are really interested in your topic.**

Julian is really interested in his topic because he is writing about his dog. He likes to share ideas about him.

My Buddy

I'm Julian, and my dog is my best buddy. Can you guess what his name is? That's right! It's Buddy.

Buddy eats strange things. He chews on rugs and bones. Once he even ate a raw fish! He smelled awful after that.

Buddy always spends time with me. Every morning, he walks me to the school bus. He's always waiting at the bus stop when I get home. At night, my best buddy sleeps on my bed.

practice

Write a story about an animal. Does your writing sound like you are really interested in your topic?

Conventions — Follow the rules for writing.

Before Mia publishes her writing, she checks for grammar, capitalization, punctuation, and spelling. She uses a rubric and a checklist to help her.

Did you check?

Grammar

 1. Did you use verbs correctly?

Capitalization

 2. Did you start each sentence with a capital letter?

✔ 3. Did you capitalize the first letter of names or proper nouns?

Punctuation

✔ 4. Did you end each sentence with the correct punctuation mark?

Spelling

 5. Did you spell all your words correctly?

TEKS 2.17A, 2.17B, 2.17C, 2.17D

Connecting the Process and the Traits

The writing process and the traits of writing work together. The chart shows that some traits are important during certain steps in the process.

Prewrite

Focus	Generate ideas and choose a topic.
Organization	Plan a beginning, middle, and end.
Ideas	Think of details about your topic.

Draft

Focus	Write about your topic.
Organization	Write your ideas in order.
Ideas	Add interesting details.
Voice	Sound interested in your topic.

Revise

Focus	Take out details that do not belong.
Organization	Move parts that seem out of order.
Ideas	Add words that are clear and specific. Rewrite any ideas that could be clearer.
Voice	Change parts that don't show interest.

Edit

Conventions	Use a rubric to check your grammar, capitalization, punctuation, and spelling.

Writing Tips

- **Talk with a Partner**

  Talking with a partner will help you gather great ideas.

- **Use Graphic Organizers**

  Graphic organizers will help you organize your ideas.

- **Think About Your Reader**

  Think of your reader to help you find the right voice.

- **Check Your Sentences**

  Make sure your sentences are clear and easy to follow.

Don't worry about the conventions too early in the process. Leave that until you have revised your writing.

Evaluating your Writing

Hana loves to look at the rabbits at the fair. Judges rate or score the rabbits according to their health and grooming. The very best rabbits get blue ribbons, and others get red or white ribbons.

Your writing can be scored, too, with a chart called a **rubric**. This chapter will show you how using a rubric can help you make your writing better.

Getting Started

Look at the rubric on pages 30–31. It shows you the conventions to include in your writing.

Read

Before you write, read the rubric column for a score of 4. This will tell you what a score of 4 should have. It will help you know how to write well.

Write

Write your first draft. Then revise your draft to improve your writing traits and edit your draft using a rubric to improve your writing conventions.

Review

Review the conventions instruction within the unit, if you need more help. You can also use the index to find certain skill instruction.

TEKS 2.17D
ELPS 1B

Using a Rubric

Rubrics can help you edit and rate your writing.

Sample Rubric

 In my writing:

- I used common and proper nouns correctly in all sentences.
- I used end punctuation for all sentences.
- I used quotation marks correctly in all sentences.
- I started all sentences with capital letters.
- I capitalized all proper nouns.
- I spelled all words correctly.

 In my writing:

- I used common and proper nouns correctly in most sentences.
- I used end punctuation for most sentences.
- I used quotation marks correctly in most sentences.
- I started most sentences with capital letters.
- I capitalized most proper nouns.
- I spelled most words correctly.

 In my writing:

- I used common and proper nouns correctly in some sentences.
- I used end punctuation for some sentences.
- I used quotation marks correctly in some sentences.
- I started some sentences with capital letters.
- I capitalized some proper nouns.
- I spelled some words correctly.

 In my writing:

- I did not use common and proper nouns correctly in any sentences.
- I did not use end punctuation for any sentences.
- I did not use quotation marks correctly in any sentences.
- I did not start any sentences with capital letters.
- I did not capitalize any proper nouns.
- I misspelled many words.

Learning Language

A **rubric** describes what each score looks like. How can a **rubric** help you make your writing better? Talk about it with a partner.

TEKS 2.17E, 2.27
ELPS 4G

Publishing and Portfolios

Publishing is **sharing** your writing. This chapter tells about ways to publish, including using a portfolio.

Ideas for Publishing

There are many ways to share your writing. Kara reads the story to her class. Denzel puts his writing on the bulletin board.

More Publishing Ideas

Act it out!   Act out your story for your class, your family, or your friends.

Bind it!   Make a book. Put your writing and pictures together in a book.

Send it!   Write an e-mail. Send it to a friend, a family member, or a classmate.

Submit it!   Send your story to magazines that publish student writing.

Display it!   With your teacher's permission, display your writing in the classroom.

Read it!   Read your writing to classmates, friends, and family. Sometimes the simplest way to publish can be the best.

Talk it over.

What other ways can you think of to share your writing?

Sharing a Handwritten Copy

When you write your final copy, remember these things.

- Use your best penmanship.
- Write on one side of your paper.
- Add a picture.

Handwritten Copy

Saturday

Saturday is the best day of the week. My family and I have breakfast together. Sometimes we have pancakes. Other times we have breakfast burritos. Then we might go shopping. Some Saturdays we go to the park to kick a ball around. It doesn't matter where we go. I love Saturdays!

Sharing a Computer Copy

When you use a computer, be sure that your writing looks neat and readable.

- Leave a one-inch margin on all sides.
- Use a font that is easy to read.
- Add a photo or a picture.

Computer Copy

↕ 1"

Saturday

Saturday is the best day of the week. My family and I have breakfast together. Sometimes we have pancakes. Other times we have breakfast burritos. Then we might go shopping. Some Saturdays we go to the park to kick a ball around. It doesn't matter where we go. I love Saturdays!

Understanding Portfolios

A **portfolio** is a special place to keep your writing. You can use a special folder for your portfolio, or you can use an electronic file on the computer. Your teacher will check your portfolio from time to time to see how you are doing.

Using a Portfolio

A portfolio can be used in many ways. Here are four important uses.

Collect You can collect ideas for new stories and poems.

Keep You can keep pictures and drawings you like.

Store You can store unfinished writing to work on later.

Save You can save final copies to read later.

Two Kinds of Portfolios

There are two main kinds of portfolios that you can create.

Showcase Portfolio

In a *showcase portfolio,* you show your best writing. Your teacher will help you decide which writing to include.

Growth Portfolio

In a *growth portfolio,* you save writing from different times of the year. You will be surprised how your writing improves.

Learning Language

A **portfolio** is a special kind of folder. Which kind of **portfolio** would you like to make? Talk about it with a partner.

Descriptive Writing

Writing Focus

- Descriptive Paragraph
- Writing Across the Curriculum

Learning Language

Work with a partner. Read the meanings and share answers to the questions.

1. A descriptive sentence describes what something looks like, sounds like, feels like, smells like, or tastes like.
   Tell your partner a descriptive sentence about your favorite animal.

2. A curriculum is a list of the subjects you study in school, such as math and science.
   What are your favorite subjects in your curriculum?

3. When something makes sense, you understand it.
   What do you do when you read something that doesn't make sense?

In descriptive writing, you use words to create a picture, or image, of a topic. You can tell what your topic looks like, sounds like, feels like, smells like, or tastes like—just by sharing the best words and details.

Writing a
Descriptive Paragraph

Isabel described her friend Marty in a descriptive paragraph. In a way, she painted a picture with words. You can make a word picture of someone you know, too! This chapter will show you how.

Isabel's Descriptive Paragraph

My Teammate Marty

Topic Sentence

My friend Marty is on my soccer team. He wears a blue baseball hat. His hair is brown, and his eyes light up when he smiles.

Body Sentences

He wears a uniform that includes a T-shirt and blue pants. Marty's white shoes wear out quickly because he runs fast and plays hard.

Closing Sentence

Marty loves playing soccer, and he is a great teammate.

- The **topic sentence** tells who the paragraph is about.
- The **body sentences** describe what the person looks like and what she or he does.
- The **closing sentence** tells how the writer feels about the person.

Prewriting ▶ Planning Your Writing

To get started you need to select an interesting topic and gather details about it.

Quick List

First, Isabel listed interesting people she knows. Then she circled the person she wanted to write about.

After Isabel chose Marty as her topic, she created a chart of details about him.

Grandma

Anita

Marty

Details Chart

Topic: Marty		
Looks like	Sounds like	Likes to do
big smile	soft voice	loves soccer
red striped shirt	giggles	runs fast
blue cap		likes popcorn

Prewrite ▶ **Choose a topic/Gather details.**

1. List three people you know well.
2. Circle one person to write about.
3. Make a details chart like the one above.
4. Draw a picture of your person, if it will help you.

Drafting ▶ Writing Your First Draft

You can use your details chart and picture to help you write your paragraph. Remember each part of your paragraph has a special job.

> Isabel wrote a topic sentence, body sentences, and a closing sentence in her paragraph. She used many ideas from her details chart.

Draft ▶ **Write your first draft.**

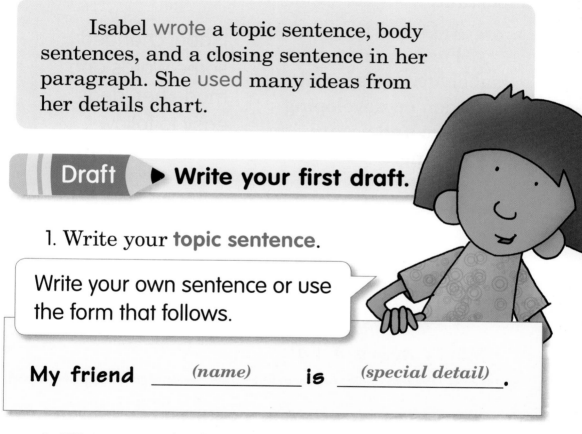

1. Write your **topic sentence**.

Write your own sentence or use the form that follows.

My friend _____*(name)*_____ **is** _____*(special detail)*_____ .

2. Write your **body sentences**. Use words and details from your chart and picture to describe the person.

3. Write your **closing sentence**. Tell how you feel about the person.

 TEKS 2.17C

Revising ▶ Improving Your Writing

Now it is time to review your writing to see if any parts need to be improved. When you revise, check for the traits your teacher feels are really important.

For her revising, Isabel focused special attention on developing her ideas and organizing her writing.

Isabel changed some words and made her ideas easy to follow.

Revise ▶ Improve your writing.

1. Use specific words to develop your ideas.

> soccer
> My friend marty is on my ∧teem.
> blue baseball
> Marty wears a ∧hat.

2. Make your writing easy to follow.

> Marty's white shoes wear out
> because
> quickly. ∧He runs fast and plays hard.

Editing ▶ Checking for Conventions

After you revise your paragraph, check it for grammar, capitalization, punctuation, and spelling. (See page 452.)

Isabel and a classmate checked her writing for conventions, using the checklist below.

Isabel's Editing

> My friend marty is on my soccer teem.
>
> He wears a blue baseball hat his hair is
>
> brown, and his eyes light up when he smiles.

Did you check?

✔ 1. Did you begin each name and sentence with a capital letter?

✔ 2. Did you end each sentence with correct punctuation?

✔ 3. Did you spell your words correctly?

 Edit ▶ **Check for errors.**

Writing
Across the Curriculum

Science or Math: A Shape Riddle

In science or math class, you may be asked to write about subjects you are studying. Ronnie wrote a shape riddle for his science class.

What Am I?

The **topic sentence** names the shape.

I am a sphere in room 213. I feel round and smooth like a ball. I am bigger than a basketball.

The **body sentences** give clues.

Some parts of me are blue. Other parts are brown or green. I have words and lines all over me. I can show you where anyone on Earth

The **closing sentence** asks the riddle question.

lives. What am I?

Answer: a globe

Writing Tips

Use these tips to write your own shape riddle.

Before You Write

Pick an object that has a special shape.

Complete a details chart about the object.

Details Chart

Topic:		
Looks like	Sounds like	Know about

During Your Writing

Name your object's shape in the topic sentence.

Give clues from your list in the body sentences.

In the closing, write your riddle question.

After You Have Written

Read your riddle to a partner. Ask if it makes sense.

Add or change details to make your riddle clear.

Correct mistakes and make a final copy.

 TEKS 2.19B

Practical Writing: An E-Mail Message

Paul wrote an e-mail message to his friend Jo. He talked about a park near his home in Texas.

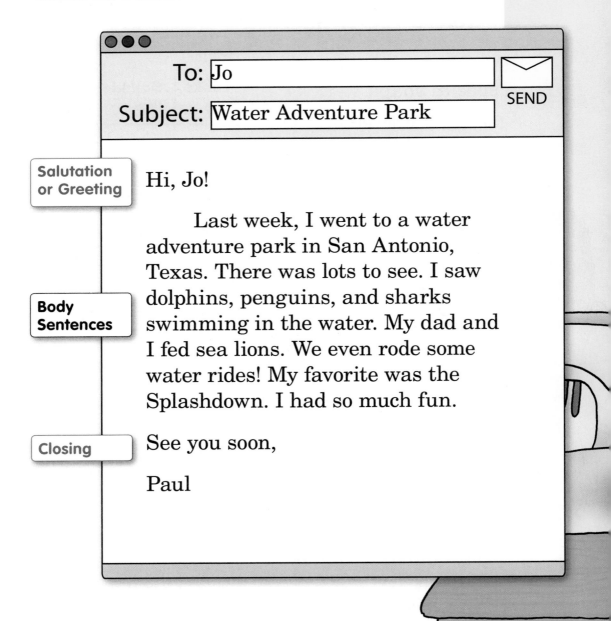

To: Jo

Subject: Water Adventure Park

SEND

Salutation or Greeting

Hi, Jo!

Body Sentences

Last week, I went to a water adventure park in San Antonio, Texas. There was lots to see. I saw dolphins, penguins, and sharks swimming in the water. My dad and I fed sea lions. We even rode some water rides! My favorite was the Splashdown. I had so much fun.

Closing

See you soon,

Paul

TEKS 2.17A, 2.17B, 2.17E, 2.19B
ELPS 5G

Writing Tips

Use these tips to write your own e-mail message.

Before You Write

Choose a person to receive your e-mail.

Pick a place to describe.

Make a sensory list to gather details.

Sensory List

See	
Hear	
Smell	
Taste	
Feel	

During Your Writing

Begin with a fun salutation or greeting.

Share ideas from your list in the body sentences.

Make your closing a friendly good-bye.

After You Have Written

Read over your e-mail. Be sure you have clearly described your place.

Correct mistakes in grammar, capitalization, punctuation, and spelling.

Send your e-mail.

ELPS 1A, 2C, 3E, 4G

Narrative Writing

TEXAS
WRITE
SOURCE
Online
www.hmheducation.com/tx/writesource

Writing Focus

- Narrative Paragraph
- Personal Narrative
- Across the Curriculum
- Assessment

Grammar Focus

- Common and Proper Nouns

Learning Language

Work with a partner. Read the meanings and share answers to the questions.

1. A time line shows events in time order.
   On a time line of your life, what event would you list first?
2. A narrative is a story.
   Tell a narrative of your day so far.
3. When you lead up to a certain part of a story, you prepare for it.
   In *Cinderella*, what events lead up to Cinderella losing her slipper?

You like to tell stories about interesting or important things that happen to you, right? When you write those stories down, they're called narratives. In a narrative, you can tell what happened two years ago or what happened just last night. This section will help you write great narratives.

Writing a
Narrative
Paragraph

The students in Colin's class talked about special experiences. They discovered many stories that they could tell about themselves, their families, and their friends. Colin remembered visiting the zoo with his brother and decided to write a narrative paragraph about it.

In this chapter, you will write a paragraph about a special experience you've had.

Colin's Narrative Paragraph

My Zoo Surprise

Topic Sentence

My big brother and I had fun at the zoo. The peacocks squawked and fanned out their tails. Prairie dogs chased each other and dived into their holes.

Body Sentences

Then we squeezed between people to get to a huge window where we could see underwater. Suddenly a polar bear crashed into the water. It pushed its nose right up to the window.

Closing Sentence

My big brother and I were nose to nose with a polar bear!

- The **topic sentence** tells the main idea of the paragraph.
- The **body sentences** tell what happened.
- The **closing sentence** gives the reader something to think about.

Prewriting ▶ Choosing Your Topic

When planning a paragraph, start by choosing an interesting topic.

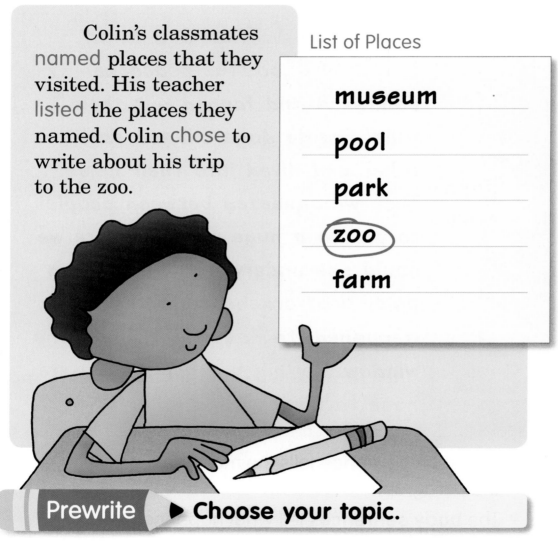

Colin's classmates named places that they visited. His teacher listed the places they named. Colin chose to write about his trip to the zoo.

List of Places

museum

pool

park

zoo

farm

Prewrite ▶ **Choose your topic.**

1. List some places you've visited.
2. Choose a place and a time to write about.

Prewriting ▶ Gathering Details

The next important step is to select details about your topic.

To gather details, Colin made a time line. He listed events in the order they happened. This is called *time order*.

Time Line

Topic: Visiting the Zoo

- I went to the zoo with my brother.
- We saw peacocks and prairie dogs.
- A polar bear jumped into the water.
- It pushed its nose up to the window.

Prewrite ▶ **Gather details.**

1. Make a time line like the one above.
2. List the main events of your story in time order.

 **TEKS** 2.17B, 2.21A(vii)
ELPS 5G

Drafting ▶ Writing Your Paragraph

Now you are ready to write your narrative paragraph. Use your time line as a guide.

First, Colin wrote a topic sentence. Then he added sentences that tell his story. He used words that show time order. Colin closed with an interesting idea.

Draft ▶ **Write your paragraph.**

1. Write the topic sentence to tell what your paragraph is about.

If you get stuck, fill in the sentence below on your paper.

I had fun with _____*(person)* at the _____*(place)*.

2. Add sentences to tell your story in order. Use time-order words like *first, next,* and *then*.

3. Close with an interesting or fun idea.

Revising and Editing

Once you finish your first draft, you are ready to revise, edit, and publish. Your goal is to make your paragraph clear and fun to read.

Colin reviewed his ideas to make sure they were in the right order. He took out ideas that did not belong. Then he checked for conventions.

Revise ▶ Improve your writing.

1. Be sure the events in your story are in the right order. Add time-order words if needed.
2. Take out any ideas that do not belong.

Edit ▶ Check for conventions.

1. Be sure that you use grammar, capital letters, and punctuation correctly. (See page 452.)
2. Also check for spelling errors.

Publish ▶ Share your writing.

Writing a
Personal Narrative

Fred helped his grandpa in a community garden. He wrote about his adventure in a personal narrative. A personal narrative uses more than one paragraph to tell about a true experience.

In this chapter, you will write a personal narrative about a place you have visited.

 # Understanding Your Goal

The traits below will help you write a personal narrative.

 Focus Write about a true experience. Make sure all of your ideas are about that experience.

 **Organization** Tell what happened in order from first to last.

 **Development of Ideas** Add interesting details to develop your story. Use a detail cluster to help you gather details.

 **Voice** Make your writing sound like you are really interested in your story.

 **Conventions** Check your writing for grammar, capital letters, punctuation, and spelling.

 Literature Connection: You can find a personal narrative in *My Name Is Gabriela* by Monica Brown.

60

Fred's Personal Narrative

My Day at the Community Garden

Beginning   My grandpa took me to the community garden. It contains rows and rows of healthy plants.

Middle   Grandpa showed me lettuce, peas, and corn. Then he showed me how to pull weeds without pulling the vegetables. It's not easy. He told me that garden work is important. He said, "People who have food need to share it." Finally, we took the food from the garden to a food bank. I felt proud working with Grandpa.

Ending   I liked the community garden. The best part was spending time with Grandpa. I learned that working together and helping others is fun.

Parts of a Personal Narrative

A personal narrative contains three main parts—the beginning, the middle, and the ending. Look at the three parts of Fred's narrative.

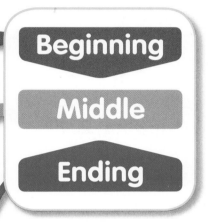

In the beginning paragraph, Fred tells which special experience he will write about.

In the middle paragraph, Fred writes about the experience.

In the ending paragraph, Fred explains what he learned and how he feels.

After You Read

1. **Focus** What experience did Fred share?
2. **Organization** How are Fred's ideas in order? What time-order words did Fred use?
3. **Ideas** Which details help develop Fred's ideas?

Prewriting ▶ Choosing a Topic

Choosing a topic is an important first step when planning a narrative. Always select a writing topic that really interests you.

Here's how Kelsey selected her topic.

List   Kelsey listed places she had been.

Circle   She then circled the topic she wanted to write about.

List of Places

hospital

Standing Rock

Navy Pier

zoo

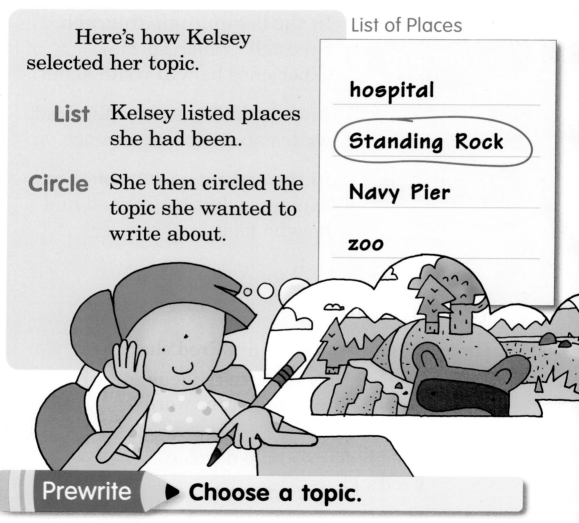

Prewrite ▶ **Choose a topic.**

1. List places you have visited.
2. Circle the place you want to write about.

Prewriting ▶ Gathering Details

Before writing, it is important to collect details about your topic.

This is how Kelsey collected her details.

Make   Kelsey made a cluster.

Name   She named her topic in the middle of her cluster. Then she added details.

Details Cluster

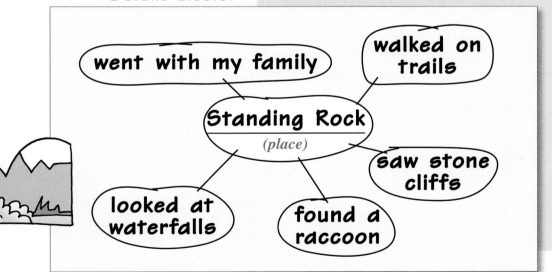

Prewrite ▶ **Gather details.**

1. Make a cluster.
2. Name your topic and add details about it.

TEKS 2.17B, 2.18A
ELPS 5G

Drafting ▶ Beginning Your Story

The beginning part of a narrative should get the reader's interest and introduce your topic.

This is what Kelsey did to write the beginning of her story.

▶ **Beginning**

Middle

Ending

Review   Kelsey reviewed the ideas in her cluster.

Write   Then Kelsey wrote a beginning sentence that introduces her topic.

> **My family went to Standing Rock state park.**

Add   Next, Kelsey wrote more sentences to help introduce her topic.

Kelsey's beginning paragraph introduces her topic and leads up to the main action in her story.

Kelsey's Beginning Paragraph

My family went to Standing Rock state park. My cousins stayed home. Waterfalls fell over the high rocks. We walked on trails through stone clifs. I saw fuzzy green stuff on the edge of the path Then I said, "I hear something really strange!"

Draft ▶ **Begin your story.**

1. Write an interesting sentence to introduce your topic.
2. Add more sentences to help introduce the topic.

TEKS 2.17B, 2.18A, 2.22C(i)
ELPS 5G

Drafting ▶ Continuing Your Story

In the middle part of your narrative, you should tell about the main action. Make this part exciting!

This is what Kelsey did to continue her story.

Beginning

▶ Middle

Ending

Review Kelsey again looked at her cluster for ideas to include in the middle part of her story.

Write Next, she wrote about the main action.

Include Kelsey included details, dialogue (talking), and personal feelings.

I used quotation marks to show that someone is talking.

In the middle paragraph, Kelsey included details, dialogue, and her personal feelings.

Kelsey's Middle Paragraph

Inside a garbage can, I found a raccoon. We see wild animals in our backyard. "There's a baby raccoon here!" I shouted. I was mad because no one beleved me. Who cared about seeing another waterfall? I wanted to help the raccoon! Dad and Mom just wanted to keep walking.

Draft ▶ Continue your story.

1. Review your cluster for ideas.
2. Write about the main action of your story.
3. Include details, personal feelings, and dialogue. (See page 466 for dialogue.)

Drafting ▶ Ending Your Story

In the ending part, you should finish your story and tell one last important thing.

This is what Kelsey did to write her ending.

Beginning
Middle
▶ **Ending**

Write Kelsey finished her story by telling how the main action ended.

Add Kelsey added her last sentence. She tried three ways to write it.

1. **Say something about yourself.**

   I learned I could be a hero!

2. **Say something about other people.**

   Park workers have an important job.

3. **State the final idea about the topic.**

   Wild animals like to be free.

Kelsey's ending paragraph completes her story and shares a final idea.

Kelsey's Ending Paragraph

> At the end of our hike, Dad looked in the garbage can and saw my raccoon! Then he found a park worker. She tipped the can and the raccoon hurried into the woods. I learned that I could be a hero!

In my last sentence, I decided to share what I learned about myself.

Draft ▸ **End your story.**

1. Write the final part to finish your story.
2. Add one more sentence to complete the narrative.

Texas Traits ★ Revising for Focus

When you revise, you try to make your writing better. First, make sure that all of your ideas are about your topic.

These are the things that Kelsey did to revise her writing for focus.

Read Kelsey read her draft. She thought about the ideas in her story.

Decide Kelsey decided if each idea was about her vacation.

Mark She removed any ideas that did not belong by using the take out (Ꝓ) editing symbol.

I took out a sentence that was not about my vacation.

Kelsey kept her focus on her vacation.

Kelsey's Revising

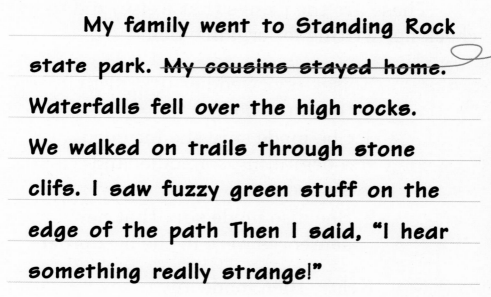

My family went to Standing Rock
state park. ~~My cousins stayed home.~~
Waterfalls fell over the high rocks.
We walked on trails through stone
clifs. I saw fuzzy green stuff on the
edge of the path Then I said, "I hear
something really strange!"

Revise ▶ Improve your focus.

1. Review your first draft for focus. Make sure all of your ideas are about your topic.
2. Mark the ideas you want to take out using the take out ( ) editing symbol.

Revising for Organization

When you revise for organization, you make sure that your ideas are in the best order.

These are the things that Kelsey did to check her writing for organization.

Review Kelsey reviewed her first draft for organization.

1. She made sure she included a beginning, a middle, and an ending.
2. She also made sure that her sentences were in the best order.

Make Kelsey then made any needed changes.

In the first paragraph, I decided to move one sentence to make my writing clearer.

Kelsey's Revising

> My family went to Standing Rock state park. ~~My cousins stayed home.~~ Waterfalls fell over the high rocks. We walked on trails through stone clifs. I saw fuzzy green stuff on the edge of the path Then I said, "I hear something really strange!"

Make sure your story is easy to follow from start to finish.

Revise ▶ **Improve your organization.**

1. Review your first draft for organization.
2. Make any needed changes.

TEKS 2.17C, 2.18A
ELPS 2I, 3E

 **Revising for** **Development of Ideas**

When you revise for ideas, you make sure that your writing has specific details about your topic.

These are the things that Kelsey did to develop the ideas in her story.

Read   Kelsey read her first draft to herself and to a partner.

> Reading your story out loud helps you find ideas that should be changed.

Listen   She listened to what her partner said about her ideas.

Make   Then Kelsey made any needed changes.

> In the beginning paragraph, I added two details to develop my ideas.

Kelsey's Revising

Last Summer

ᴧ My family went to Standing Rock state park. ~~My cousins stayed home.~~

Waterfalls fell over the high rocks.

We walked on trails through stone clifs. I saw fuzzy green *moss* ᴧ stuff on the edge of the path Then I said, "I hear something really strange!"

Revise ▶ **Improve your ideas.**

1. Read your first draft to yourself and to a partner.
2. Listen to what your partner says about your ideas.
3. Make any needed changes.

TEKS 2.17C, 2.18A
ELPS 3E

Revising for Voice

When you revise for voice, you make sure that you sound interested in your topic. If you write about something personal, your writing should sound like you.

Here's what Kelsey did to check her writing for voice.

Read Kelsey reread her first draft. Then she asked herself two questions:

> 1. Do I sound interested in my story?
> 2. Does my writing show my personality?

Ask Kelsey also asked her friend to check her narrative for voice.

Make Then she made any needed changes.

> I changed some words to help my writing sound more like myself.

Kelsey's Revising

> Last Summer ^ parents and I
> ^ My family went to Standing Rock
>
> state park. ~~My cousins stayed home.~~
>
> Waterfalls fell over the high rocks.
>
> We walked on trails through stone
>
> clifs. I saw fuzzy green ~~stuff~~ moss on the
>
> edge of the path Then I ~~said,~~ yelled "I hear
>
> something really strange!"

Make sure you sound excited about your story.

Revise ▸ **Improve your voice.**

1. Read your first draft to be sure that you sound interested in your topic.
2. Ask your teacher or friend to check your writing.
3. Make any needed changes.

TEKS 2.21A(ii)
ELPS 2C, 3E, 4C

Editing for Conventions

Grammar

When you edit for grammar, you make sure you use words correctly.

What is a noun?

A **noun** names a person, place, or thing. Look at the sentences below. The words in red are nouns.

The **park** has a **slide**.

The **girl** plays there.

Grammar Practice

Talk It Over With a partner, make a list of nouns. Use the nouns to fill in the blanks below. Then read your silly paragraph!

My _____(person)_____ gave me a gift. It is a blue _____(thing)_____. It looks like a _____(thing)_____. I play with it at the _____(place)_____. I want to give one to my _____(person)_____.

What are common and proper nouns?

A **common noun** names any person, place, or thing. A **proper noun** names a specific person, place, or thing. A proper noun starts with a capital letter.

Common Noun	Proper Noun
boy	Miguel
city	Dallas
park	Custer Park

Grammar Practice

Talk It Over With a partner, read the sentences. Decide if each underlined noun is common or proper. Then rewrite each sentence using the correct capitalization.

1. This <u>summer</u> we visited <u>chicago</u>.
2. My <u>cousin</u> <u>eric</u> lives there.
3. We stayed in a <u>hotel</u>.
4. One <u>day</u>, we went to <u>lake michigan</u>.

Learning Language

Play a noun game with a partner. Say a common noun, such as *man*. Then have your partner say a proper noun that goes with it, such as *Mr. Lee*. Take turns naming common and proper nouns.

TEKS 2.18A, 2.21A(ii), 2.22B(i), 2.22C(i)
ELPS 1B, 3E, 5C

Editing for Conventions

After revising your first draft, it's time to check for grammar, capitalization, punctuation, and spelling. (See page 452.)

These are the things that Kelsey did to edit her writing for conventions.

Check Kelsey checked her story for conventions. She used the rubric on pages 82–83 as a guide. Then she asked a classmate to check her story for conventions.

Mark Then Kelsey marked her errors and corrected them.

Did you check?

✓ 1. Did you capitalize the first word of each sentence and proper nouns?

✓ 2. Did you use punctuation at the end of each sentence?

✓ 3. Did you add quotation marks around a speaker's words? (See page 466.)

✓ 4. Did you spell your words correctly?

Kelsey's Editing

> Last summer, my parents and I
> went to Standing Rock state park. We
> walked on trails through stone clifs.
> Waterfalls fell over the high rocks. I
> saw fuzzy green moss on the edge
> of the path Then I yelled, "I hear
> something really strange!"

I added capital letters to the name of a place, corrected a spelling error, and added a period.

Edit ▶ Check for conventions.

1. Check your story for conventions using the rubric on pages 82–83.
2. Ask a partner to check for conventions, too.
3. Mark any errors and correct them.

TEKS 2.17D, 2.18A, 2.21A(ii), 2.22B(i), 2.22C(i)
ELPS 1B, 5C

Editing Using a Rubric

Use this rubric while you edit to improve your writing. Remember, when you edit, you make sure that you have followed the rules for grammar, sentence structure, capitalization, punctuation, and spelling.

In my writing:

- I used common and proper nouns correctly in all sentences.
- I used end punctuation for all sentences.
- I used quotation marks correctly in all sentences.
- I started all sentences with capital letters.
- I capitalized all proper nouns.
- I spelled all words correctly.

In my writing:

- I used common and proper nouns correctly in most sentences.
- I used end punctuation for most sentences.
- I used quotation marks correctly in most sentences.
- I started most sentences with capital letters.
- I capitalized most proper nouns.
- I spelled most words correctly.

I use a rubric when I edit. It helps me improve my writing!

2 In my writing:

- I used common and proper nouns correctly in some sentences.

- I used end punctuation for some sentences.

- I used quotation marks correctly in some sentences.

- I started some sentences with capital letters.

- I capitalized some proper nouns.

- I spelled some words correctly.

1 In my writing:

- I did not use common and proper nouns correctly in any sentences.

- I did not use end punctuation for any sentences.

- I did not use quotation marks correctly in any sentences.

- I did not start any sentences with capital letters.

- I did not capitalize any proper nouns.

- I misspelled many words.

TEKS 2.17E
ELPS 3E

Publishing ▶ Sharing Your Narrative

Standing Rock State Park

Last summer, my parents and I went to Standing Rock State Park. We walked on trails through stone cliffs. Waterfalls fell over the high rocks. I saw fuzzy green moss on the edge of the path. Then I yelled, "I hear something really strange!"

Inside a garbage can, I found a raccoon. "There's a baby raccoon here!" I shouted. Dad and Mom just wanted to keep walking. I was mad because no one believed me. Who cared about seeing another waterfall? I wanted to help the raccoon!

At the end of our hike, Dad looked in the garbage can and saw my raccoon! Then Dad found a park ranger. She tipped the can over, and the raccoon hurried into the woods. I learned that I could be a hero!

Publish ▶ **Share your narrative.**

Reflecting on Your Writing

After you finish your narrative, take some time to think about it. Then fill in a sheet like this about your story.

Thinking About Your Writing

Name: __Kelsey__

Title: __Standing Rock State Park__

1. The best thing about my narrative is

   __remembering the baby raccoon in__

   __the garbage can.__

2. The main thing I learned while writing

   my narrative is __that proper nouns__

   __get a capital letter.__

 **TEKS** 2.19B, 2.22B(iii)

Writing
Across the Curriculum

Social Studies: A Community Helper

For social studies, Josie wrote a letter about a community helper. She sent it to her school principal.

Date	October 3, 2010
Salutation or Greeting	Dear Mr. Sanchez,
Body Sentences	Ms. Stein is a great crossing guard! This morning, I was waiting for Ms. Stein to let me cross when a puppy ran into the street. Ms. Stein told me to stay where I was. She stepped into the street and held up her stop sign. All the cars stopped, and Ms. Stein picked up the puppy. We should all be happy to have Ms. Stein in our community.
Closing	Sincerely,
Signature	Josie Jimenez

Writing Tips

Use these tips to write your own letter.

Before You Write

List some community helpers.

Think about an experience you shared with one of them.

Use a time line to gather details about the experience.

Time Line

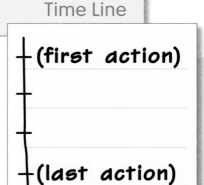

┼ (first action)

┼

┼

┼ (last action)

During Your Writing

Begin with the date and the greeting.

Tell about the experience in order.

Use a respectful closing like **Sincerely** and sign your name.

After You Have Written

Check for the parts of a letter.

Add or change any ideas to make them clearer.

Correct any errors and make a neat final copy.

Music: A Personal Story

For music class, Richard wrote a story about playing in a family band. The band played zydeco music.

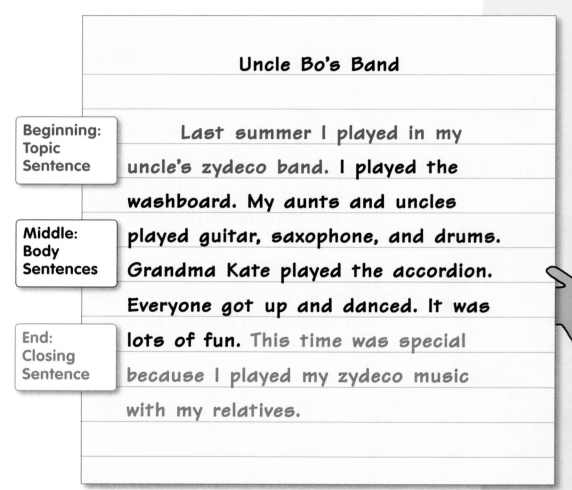

Uncle Bo's Band

Beginning: Topic Sentence

Middle: Body Sentences

End: Closing Sentence

Last summer I played in my uncle's zydeco band. I played the washboard. My aunts and uncles played guitar, saxophone, and drums. Grandma Kate played the accordion. Everyone got up and danced. It was lots of fun. This time was special because I played my zydeco music with my relatives.

Writing Tips

Use these tips to write your own music story.

Before You Write

List experiences you have had with music.

Choose one of the times to write about.

Use a cluster to gather details about the experience.

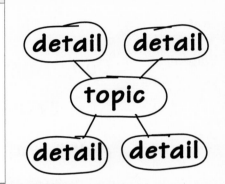

During Your Writing

Beginning: Name the experience in the topic sentence.

Middle: Tell what happened in the body sentences.

End: Share how you felt in the closing sentence.

After You Have Written

Review your paragraph.

Make sure you wrote about one special time.

Check for conventions.

Practical Writing: A Thank-You Letter

Daniel wrote a letter to his aunt to thank her for a birthday gift.

Date

July 23, 2011

Salutation or Greeting

Dear Aunt Elena,

Body Sentences

Thank you so much for the giant water cannon. I am having so much fun with it! My sisters don't like it, but I enjoy sneaking up on them. My neighbor has the same kind of water cannon, and we like to play with them all day.

I hope you can visit us soon. I promise not to get you wet!

Closing

Love,

Signature

Daniel

Writing Tips

Use these tips to write your own thank-you letter.

Before You Write

Think of the gift.

Answer the 5 W questions.
    Who gave you the gift?
    What is the gift?
    When and **where** do
    you use it?
    Why do you like it?

5 W's Chart

Who?	
What?	
When?	
Where?	
Why?	

During Your Writing

Start with the date and the greeting.

Answer the 5 W's in the body sentences.

Use a friendly closing like **Love** or **Your friend** and sign your name.

After You Have Written

Review your letter.

Change any parts that could be improved.

Check for conventions and parts of a letter.

Writing for Assessment

On most writing tests, you will read a **prompt** and write a paragraph about it.

Writing Prompt

Remember something you did for the first time. Write a paragraph about the time.

Think After Zane read the prompt, he thought about things that he'd done for the first time.

List He listed a few of those experiences.

Choose Zane chose the experience he wanted to write about and circled it.

List of Experiences

trampoline
high board
soccer goal

Zane's Narrative Paragraph

My High Jump

The **topic sentence** names the topic.

The **body sentences** tell what happened.

The **closing sentence** shares a feeling.

   Last summer, Aunt Shandi took me to a pool. **Kids in the water were splashing, swimming, and yelling. Then I saw the high diving board. I'd never used it before, but Aunt Shandi said I could jump. I climbed up the big ladder. The water looked a long way down. I took a deep breath and jumped. Down I went. The water made a great big splash around me.** My jump was great!

practice

1. List first-time experiences.
2. Write a paragraph about one of your first-time experiences.

 Literature Connection: You can find narrative writing in *Luke Goes to Bat* by Rachel Isadora.

ELPS 1A, 2C, 3E, 4G

Expository Writing

Writing Focus

- Expository Paragraph
- Expository Letter
- Across the Curriculum
- Assessment

Grammar Focus

- Verb tenses

Learning Language

Work with a partner. Read the meanings and share answers to the questions.

1. **Directions** tell how to do something.
   Give directions for making a snack.
2. **Chronological** order is the order in which things happen. It is time order.
   List something in chronological order.
3. When you **make sure** to do something, you are careful to remember to do it.
   What must you make sure to do before going to sleep?

Expository writing is writing that explains or gives information. Reports, recipes, and invitations are examples of expository writing. In this section, you will write directions, a how-to letter, a classroom report, and an invitation. To do your best work, be sure to know a lot about each of your topics.

TEKS 2.19A
ELPS 5G

Writing an
Expository
Paragraph

Directions come in all shapes and sizes. You find directions in cookbooks. You also find them to help you make models or play new games.

To help a new student, Max and his classmates wrote directions to different places in their school. You can write directions, too. This chapter will show you how.

Max's Expository Paragraph

How to Find the Lunchroom

Topic Sentence

It is easy to get from our classroom to the lunchroom. **First, you leave our classroom and turn left. Walk past the office. Then**

Body Sentences

go to the trophy case, turn right, and stop. Look straight ahead of you to the end of the hall. What

Closing Sentence

do you see? You've found the lunchroom!

- The **topic sentence** introduces the topic.
- The **body sentences** give step-by-step directions.
- The **closing sentence** restates the main idea.

Prewriting ▸ Choosing a Topic

When planning an expository paragraph, begin by selecting a topic that you really want to write about.

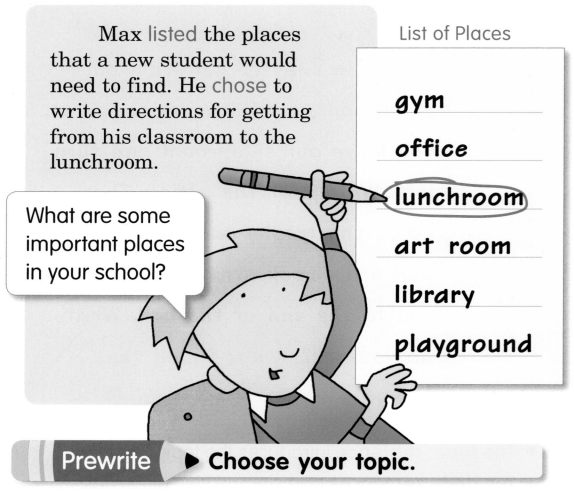

Max listed the places that a new student would need to find. He chose to write directions for getting from his classroom to the lunchroom.

What are some important places in your school?

List of Places

gym

office

lunchroom

art room

library

playground

Prewrite ▸ Choose your topic.

1. List several places in your school.
2. Choose one place for writing directions.

Prewriting ▶ Gathering Details

After you select a topic, gather details about it for your directions.

Max drew a map to help him remember details for his directions. His map shows how to get from his classroom to the lunchroom. He added labels to make his map clear.

Map

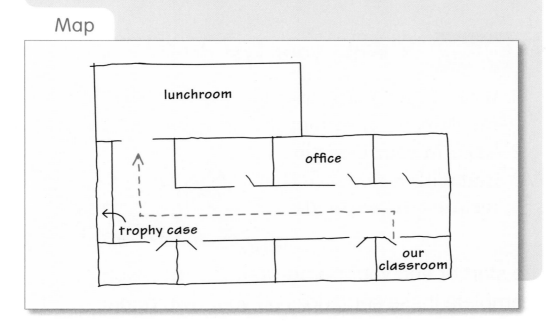

Prewrite ▶ **Gather your details.**

1. Draw a map that shows the route from your classroom to the place you chose.
2. Label at least one place you pass on the way.

 **TEKS** 2.17B, 2.19A
ELPS 5G

Drafting ▶ Writing the First Draft

Now you are ready to write your expository paragraph. Be sure to use your map as a guide.

First, Max wrote a topic sentence that names the topic. He then explained his directions in order. He ended with a sentence that finishes the directions.

Draft ▶ Write your first draft.

1. Write your topic sentence to introduce your topic.
2. Explain your directions.
3. End with a sentence that restates the main idea.

To start or end your paragraph, you may want to complete these sentences on your own paper.

To Start ▶ **This is how to get to the _____ *(place)* from the _____*(place)*_____ .**

To End ▶ **You found the _____ *(place)* _____ !**

Revising and Editing

Once you finish your first draft, you are ready to revise and edit it. Your goal is to make your directions easy to follow.

Max first made sure that he included all the directions in the right order. Then Max checked his paragraph for conventions.

Revise ▶ Improve your writing.

1. Be sure that your directions are complete and in the right order.
2. Add any ideas that are needed. Take out any ideas that do not belong.

Edit ▶ Check your conventions.

1. Be sure that you use grammar, capital letters, and punctuation correctly. (See page 452.)
2. Check for spelling errors.

> Remember to indent the first line in your paragraph.

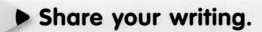 **Publish** ▶ Share your writing.

TEKS 2.19B
ELPS 5G

Writing an
Expository Letter

Emily likes to string beads. Maria knows how to grow flowers, and Ty flies kites. Everyone has a special activity that is enjoyable. What do you enjoy doing?

In this chapter, you will write an expository letter in which you explain how to do something.

Understanding Your Goal

The traits below will help you write an expository letter.

Focus — Write about how to do something. Leave out extra information.

Organization — Put the steps in the right order. Use pictures to help you.

Development of Ideas — Use interesting details to develop your topic.

Voice — Be sure that you sound interested and confident.

Conventions — Check for the parts of a letter, grammar, capitalization, punctuation, and spelling.

 Literature Connection: You can find an expository article in *How to Make a Kite* by Joanna Korba.

TEKS 2.17B, 2.19B, 2.21A(vii)

Ty's Expository Letter

Date	September 26, 2010

Salutation or Greeting

Dear Maria,

Body

Do you want to fly a kite? You will need a kite, a kite tail, string, and a windy day. You should also find a big, open place to fly your kite.

First, stand with your back to the wind. Next, have a friend hold up the kite. When the wind blows, your friend should let go of the kite. Then run fast and let out some string.

I think flying a kite is the best! I hope you like it, too.

Closing

Your pal,

Signature

Ty

Parts of a Letter

A friendly letter has five parts.

Date	A letter begins with the date.
Greeting or Salutation	The salutation or greeting is a polite way of saying, "Hi."
Body	The body is the main part of the letter. It has a beginning, middle, and end.
Closing	The closing is a polite way of saying, "Good-bye."
Signature	The signature tells who wrote the letter.

After You Read

1. **Organization** What words did Ty use to put the steps in order?

2. **Ideas** What details teach you how to fly a kite? Name two.

3. **Voice** Does Ty really like his topic? Find a sentence that shows Ty's interest.

⭐ TEKS 2.17A, 2.24A

Prewriting ▶ Choosing a Topic

To get started, choose a topic that you like and can explain. Then decide who your audience will be.

First, Maria and her class generated a list of activities. Then Maria selected a topic for her expository letter.

List of Activities

List   Maria's class listed activities they enjoy.

Circle   Maria circled the activity she wanted to write about and chose an audience.

> wash my dog
>
> grow a flower
>
> play soccer
>
> draw
>
> ride bikes

Prewrite ▶ Choose your topic.

1. Generate a list of activities you like to do.
2. Circle the topic you want to explain in a letter.
3. Decide who your audience will be.

Prewriting ▶ Gathering Details

To explain your activity, you will need to think of the steps needed to complete it. Be sure that you put the steps in chronological order.

Here's what Maria did to collect details for her expository letter.

Draw   Maria drew pictures of the steps, checked their order, and numbered each step.

Add   Finally, Maria added words for each step.

Step-by-Step Pictures

1. pot
2. dirt
3. seeds
4. sun
   water
5. sprout
6. flower

Prewrite ▶ **Gather details.**

1. Draw a picture of each step.
2. Put the steps in order and number them.
3. Add words for each step.

TEKS 2.19B
ELPS 5G

Drafting ▶ Beginning Your Letter

The beginning of your letter should have the date, the greeting or salutation, and the first paragraph of the body. The paragraph should introduce your topic and name the supplies needed.

This is what Maria did to write the beginning of her letter.

▶ **Beginning**

Middle

Ending

Review   Maria reviewed her pictures.

Introduce   Maria wrote the date and the greeting. Then she tried two ways to introduce her topic.

> 1. **Ask a question about the activity.**
>
>   **Would you like to grow a flower?**

> 2. **Make a statement about the activity.**
>
>   **I can teach you how to grow a flower.**

Add   Maria's next sentences named the supplies needed for the activity.

Maria's letter begins with the date, the greeting or salutation, and an introduction.

Maria's Beginning Paragraph

October 1, 2010

Dear Ty,

I can teach you how to grow a flower. you need a pot, potting soil, a flower seed, water, and sunlight.

My first sentence makes a statement about my activity.

Draft ▶ **Begin your letter.**

1. Review your pictures.
2. Start with the date and a salutation or greeting.
3. Introduce the topic and list the supplies needed.

TEKS 2.17B, 2.19B, 2.21A(vii)
ELPS 5G

Drafting ▶ **Writing the Middle Part**

In the middle part of your letter, you explain the steps to complete your activity. Be sure to use **time-order words** to make the steps easy to follow.

This is what Maria did to write the middle part of her letter.

Beginning
▶ Middle
Ending

Look   Maria looked again at her pictures for ideas to include in her writing.

Explain   Next, she explained the steps needed to complete the activity.

Include   Maria included time-order words like *next, then, now,* and *soon.*

Use your pictures as a guide as you write.

In the middle paragraph, Maria explained how to do her activity. She used the time-order words.

Maria's Middle Paragraph

Time-Order Words

Put some potting soil in the clay pot. Next, plant a seed. My brother always makes a mess when he plants seeds. Give the seed a little water every day Soon, a tiny, green plant will grow. Be sure it gets sunlight and water. A flower will bloum.

Draft ▶ Develop the middle part.

1. Look at your pictures.
2. Explain the steps to complete the activity.
3. Include time-order words to connect the steps.

TEKS 2.19B
ELPS 5G

Drafting ▶ Ending Your Letter

In the ending paragraph, state why you like the activity. Then give reasons to explain the statement. End your letter with a closing and a signature.

This is what Maria did to write her ending paragraph.

Beginning

Middle

▶ Ending

Write   Maria tried two ways to start this paragraph.

1. **Tell why you like the activity.**

   I like growing flowers because they are pretty.

2. **Tell why others might like this activity.**

   Growing flowers is a colorful hobby.

Choose   Maria chose the best way.

Add   Maria added two reasons that explain her choice. Then she added her closing and signature.

Maria stated why she enjoys the activity. Then she included reasons to explain the statement.

Maria's Ending Paragraph

I like growing flowers because they are pretty. It is fun to watch them grow. When they bloum, I pick them for my mom.

Your friend,
Maria

Try to give two strong reasons.

Draft ▶ **End your letter.**

1. Write a sentence that tells why you like the activity or why the reader might like it.
2. Add two or three good reasons to explain why.
3. End your letter with a closing and a signature.

Revising for Focus

When you revise, you try to make your writing better. First, make sure that all of your ideas are about your topic.

These are the things that Maria did to revise her letter for focus.

Read   Maria read her first draft to herself. She thought about the ideas in her letter.

Decide   Maria decided if each idea was about how to grow a flower.

Mark   She removed any ideas that did not belong by using the take out (⤴) editing symbol.

> I took out the sentence that was not about how to grow a flower.

Maria's Revising

> October 1, 2010
>
> Dear Ty,
>
> I can teach you how to grow a flower. you need a pot, potting soil, a flower seed, water, and sunlight.
>
> Put some potting soil in the clay pot. Next, plant a seed. ~~My brother always makes a mess when he plants seeds.~~ Give the seed a little water every day Soon, a tiny, green plant will grow. Be sure it gets sunlight and water. A flower will bloum.

Revise ▶ Improve your focus.

1. Review your first draft for focus. Make sure all of your ideas are about your topic.
2. Mark the ideas you want to take out using the take out (◞) editing symbol.

TEKS 2.17C, 2.19B, 2.21A(vii)
ELPS 1B, 3E

Revising for Organization

When you revise for organization, you make sure your ideas are in the correct order and easy to follow.

Here's what Maria did to put her writing in the best order for improved organization.

Review Maria reviewed her first draft for organization. She asked herself two questions:

> 1. Did I put the steps in the right order?
> 2. Did I use time-order words to connect the steps?

Ask Maria also asked a classmate to check her letter for organization.

Make Then she made the needed changes.

> I added two time-order words to make the steps easier to follow.

Maria's Revising

> October 1, 2010
>
> Dear Ty,
>
>   I can teach you how to grow a flower. you need a pot, potting soil, a flower seed, water, and sunlight.
>
>   First, Put some potting soil in the clay pot. Next, plant a seed. ~~My brother~~ ~~always makes a mess when he plants~~ ~~seeds.~~ Give the seed a little water every day Soon, a tiny, green plant will grow. Be sure it gets sunlight and water. Finally, A flower will bloum.

Revise ▶ **Improve your organization.**

1. Review your first draft. Are your steps in order? Did you use time-order words?
2. Ask a classmate to check your writing for organization. Make any needed changes.

TEKS 2.17C, 2.19B
ELPS 2I, 3E, 4G

Revising for Development of Ideas

When you revise for ideas, you make sure your ideas make sense. You also add interesting details.

These are the things that Maria did to develop the ideas in her letter.

Read   Maria read her first draft to herself and to a partner.

Listen   She listened to what her partner said about her ideas.

Make   Then Maria made the needed changes.

I added one detail in each paragraph. In the second paragraph, I made an idea clearer.

Maria's Revising

October 1, 2010

Dear Ty,

    I can teach you how to grow a flower. you need a ∧clay pot, potting soil, a flower seed, water, and sunlight.

    ∧First, Put some potting soil in the clay pot. Next, ∧plant ~~a seed~~ poke a flower seed down into the soil. ~~My brother always makes a mess when he plants seeds.~~ Give the seed a little water every day Soon, a tiny, green plant will grow. Be sure it gets sunlight and water. ∧Finally, A ∧pretty flower will bloum.

Revise ▶ Improve your ideas.

1. Read your first draft to yourself and a partner. Make sure your ideas are clear and detailed.
2. Listen to what your partner says about your ideas.
3. Make any needed changes.

TEKS 2.17C, 2.19B
ELPS 1B, 3E

Revising for Voice

When you revise for voice, you make sure that you sound confident and excited about your topic. If you know a lot about your topic, your writing should have voice.

Here's what Maria did to check her writing for voice.

Read Maria reread her first draft. She asked herself two questions:

> 1. Do I sound confident in every part?
> 2. Do I sound excited about the activity?

Ask Maria also asked her teacher to check her letter for voice.

Make Then she made any needed changes.

> I added a sentence that helps me sound more confident.

Maria's Revising

> October 1, 2010
>
> Dear Ty,
>
>   I can teach you how to grow a
> _clay_
> flower. you need a ∧pot, potting soil,
> _Then just follow these steps._
> a flower seed, water, and sunlight.∧
>   _First,_
>   ∧Put some potting soil in the clay
> _poke a flower seed down into the soil._
> pot. Next, ∧~~plant a seed.~~ ~~My brother~~
> ~~always makes a mess when he plants~~
> ~~seeds.~~ Give the seed a little water
> every day Soon, a tiny, green plant
> will grow. Be sure it gets sunlight and
>   _Finally,_
> water. ∧A ∧flower will bloum.
>   _pretty_

Revise ▶ Improve your voice.

1. Reread your first draft to be sure that you sound confident and excited about your topic.
2. Ask your teacher to check your writing for voice.
3. Make any needed changes.

TEKS 2.21A(i)
ELPS 3E

Grammar

When you edit for grammar, you make sure you use words correctly.

What is a verb?

A **verb** tells what action is being done. Look at the sentences below. The words in red are verbs.

The dog **barks** at night.

My teacher **sings** during class.

I **see** a butterfly.

Talk It Over With a partner, find the verb in each sentence. Take turns acting out the verb.

1. I hear thunder
2. My dog runs under the bed.
3. My baby sister cries.
4. The wind blows loudly.
5. A tree bends.
6. Raindrops splash on the roof.

What are verb tenses?

The **tense** of a verb tells if the action happens in the present, past, or future.

Present tense: The action is happening now.

I **plant** vegetables.

Past Tense: The action has already happened.

I **planted** vegetables yesterday.

Future Tense: The action will happen in the future.

I **will plant** vegetables next spring.

Talk It Over For each verb below, make up a sentence and say it to a partner. Tell if the verb is in present, past, or future tense.

1. walk   2. saved   3. will go
4. talked   5. will sing   6. reads

Learning Language

Most past tense verbs end in –*ed*, but some verbs do not follow this rule. With a partner, read the **irregular verbs** below. Use each one in a sentence.

Present Tense	Past Tense
grow	grew
begin	began
write	wrote

TEKS 2.19B, 2.21A(i), 2.22B(i), 2.22C(i)
ELPS 1B, 3E, 5C, 5D

Texas Traits

Editing for Conventions

After revising your first draft, it's time to check it for grammar, capitalization, punctuation, and spelling. (See page 452.)

These are the things that Maria did to edit her letter for conventions.

Check Maria checked for conventions using the sample letter on page 441 and the rubric on pages 126–127 as a guide.

Ask She also asked a classmate to check her letter for conventions.

Mark Then Maria marked her errors and corrected them. You can see her changes on the next page.

Did you check?

✓ 1. Did you use verb tenses correctly?

✓ 2. Did you capitalize names and the first word of each sentence?

✓ 3. Did you use punctuation at the end of each sentence?

✓ 4. Did you spell your words correctly?

Maria's Editing

October 1, 2010

Dear Ty,

I can teach you how to grow a
flower. <u>Y</u>ou _∧**will** need a clay pot, potting soil,
a flower seed, water, and sunlight. Then
just follow these steps.

First, put some potting soil in the
clay pot. Next, poke a flower seed down
into the soil. Give the seed a little water
every day_∧ Soon, a tiny, green plant will
grow. Be sure it gets sunlight and water.
Finally, a pretty flower will ⟨**bloum**⟩ *bloom*.

Edit ▶ Check for conventions.

1. Use pages 441 and 126 to check for conventions.
2. Ask a partner to check for conventions, too.
3. Mark any errors and correct them.

TEKS 2.17D, 2.19B, 2.21A(i), 2.22B(i), 2.22B(ii), 2.22B(iii)
ELPS 1B, 5C, 5D

Texas Traits

Editing Using a Rubric

Use this rubric while you edit to improve your writing. Remember when you edit, you make sure that you have followed the rules for grammar, sentence structure, capitalization, punctuation, and spelling.

 In my writing:

- I included all parts of a letter.
- I used the correct verb tenses in all sentences.
- I used end punctuation for all sentences.
- I started all sentences with capital letters.
- I capitalized all proper names.
- I capitalized all of these letter parts: date, greeting or salutation, and closing.
- I spelled all words correctly.

 In my writing:

- I included most parts of a letter.
- I used the correct verb tenses in most sentences.
- I used end punctuation for most sentences.
- I started most sentences with capital letters.
- I capitalized most proper names.
- I capitalized two of these letter parts: date, greeting or salutation, and closing.
- I spelled most words correctly.

> I use a rubric when I edit. It helps me improve my writing!

 In my writing:

- I included some parts of a letter.
- I used the correct verb tenses in some sentences.
- I used end punctuation for some sentences.
- I started some sentences with capital letters.
- I capitalized some proper names.
- I capitalized one of these letter parts: date, greeting or salutation, and closing.
- I spelled some words correctly.

 In my writing:

- I did not include any parts of a letter.
- I did not use the correct verb tenses in any sentences.
- I did not use end punctuation for any sentences.
- I did not start any sentences with capital letters.
- I did not capitalize any proper names.
- I did not capitalize any letter parts.
- I misspelled many words.

 TEKS 2.17E, 2.19B
ELPS 3E

Publishing ▶ Sharing Your Letter

Maria's How-To Letter

October 1, 2010

Dear Ty,

    I can teach you how to grow a flower. You will need a clay pot, potting soil, a flower seed, water, and sunlight. Then just follow these steps.

    First, put some potting soil in the clay pot. Next, poke a flower seed down into the soil. Give the seed a little water every day. Soon, a tiny, green plant will grow. Be sure it gets sunlight and water. Finally, a pretty flower will bloom.

    I like growing flowers because they are pretty. It is fun to watch them grow. When they bloom, I pick them for my mom.

Your friend,
Maria

Publish ▶ **Share your letter.**

Reflecting on Your Writing

After you finish your how-to letter, take some time to think about it. Then fill in a sheet like this about your letter.

Thinking About Your Writing

Name: _Maria_

Topic: _How to Grow a Flower_

1. The best thing about my letter is

   that I put the steps in the

   right order.

2. The main thing I learned while writing

   my letter is _that it is important to_

   sound confident.

Writing
Across the Curriculum

Science: An Animal Report

In her science class, Kelli wrote an expository essay about warthogs.

Warthogs

Beginning

    Warthogs look like hairy pigs. They have tusks, long legs, and warts on their faces. Sometimes, birds sit on their backs. The birds eat bugs on the warthog.

Middle

    What do you think warthogs eat? They eat grass and seeds. They also like berries, bark, and roots. Warthogs will even eat bugs and dead animals!

Ending

    Warthogs live in Africa. They hide in aardvark tunnels. When predators come along, warthogs charge at them with their sharp tusks. Stay away from warthogs!

Writing Tips

Use these tips to write your own animal report.

Before You Write

Generate a list of animals with your class.
Choose one animal.
Read about the animal and answer these questions.

Gathering Questions

Animal:

1. What does it look like?

2. What does it eat?

3. Where does it live?

During Your Writing

Name the animal and tell what it looks like in the beginning.
Explain what it eats in the middle.
Describe where it lives in the ending.

After You Have Written

Revise your writing.
Check for grammar, capitalization, punctuation, and spelling errors.
Make a neat final copy.

TEKS 2.19B

Practical Writing: An Invitation

In class, Paulo wrote an invitation. He asked his aunt to come to a special event at his school.

Date

November 4, 2010

Salutation or Greeting

Dear Aunt Rosa,

Body Sentences

Our class is having a play to celebrate Thanksgiving. It will be in Room 44 on November 24. The play begins at two o'clock. I will be a Pilgrim in the play. We will show how the Pilgrims made their Thanksgiving dinner. Let me know if you can come.

Closing

Love,

Signature

Paulo

Writing Tips

Use these tips to write your own invitation.

Before You Write

Think of a special event.

Answer the 5 W questions .
  Who is holding the event?
  What is the event?
  When and **where** will it be?
  Why should people attend?

5 W's Chart

Who?	
What?	
When?	
Where?	
Why?	

During Your Writing

Begin with the date and the greeting.
Answer the 5 W's in the body sentences.
Write your sentences in a logical order.
Use a closing and sign your name.

After You Have Written

Change any parts that could be improved.
Correct any errors and make a neat copy.

TEKS 2.19B

Practical Writing: A Letter

Cecilia wrote a letter to her friend Greta. She explained how to make bubble mix.

Date

October 12, 2011

Salutation or Greeting

Dear Greta,

Body Sentences

Thank you for visiting last Saturday! We had fun making bubbles, didn't we? In case you don't remember, here is how we made the bubble mix.

First, get half a cup of dishwashing soap. Then gently mix in 4 cups of water. Add a few drops of corn syrup to make the bubbles strong.

Have fun making bubbles!

Closing

Your friend,

Signature

Cecilia

Writing Tips

Use these tips to write your own how-to letter.

Before You Write

Think of something you know how to do.

List the steps in a sequence chart.

Sequence Chart

First	
Next	
Then	
Last	

During Your Writing

Begin with the date and the greeting.

Follow the sequence chart to write the body sentences.

Close with **Love** or **Your friend**. Then sign your name.

After You Have Written

Review your letter and change anything that could be improved.

Check for conventions and the parts of a letter.

Make a neat final copy.

TEKS 2.17A, 2.19A
ELPS 5G

Writing for Assessment

On most writing tests, you will read a **prompt** and write a paragraph about it.

Writing Prompt

Think of a game you like to play. Write a paragraph that explains how to play it. Tell why you like the game.

Think   Yoshi thought about games he has played.

List   He listed some and circled the one he wanted to write about.

Draw   Then Yoshi drew a picture to help him write his paragraph.

List of Ideas

Games I like to play

   kickball

   (snail)

   baseball

Yoshi's Drawing

Yoshi's How-To Paragraph

Learn to Play Snail

The **topic sentence** names the game.	I know a game called snail. **First, you draw a big snail on the sidewalk. Give the snail an open mouth and a huge stomach.**
The **body sentences** tell how to play the game.	**Then put a small stone into the snail's mouth. Hop on one foot and try to kick the stone into the stomach and back to the mouth. If you do it, you get one point. If you touch a line, you don't get a point. Each player gets five turns. The player with the most points wins.** I love this
The **closing sentence** gives a final idea.	game because it is fun to hop.

practice

1. Make a list of games you play. Choose your topic.
2. Draw a picture and write your paragraph.

 Literature Connection: You can find a how-to story in *Grow a Bean Plant!* by Jennifer Duffy.

ELPS 1A, 2C, 2G, 3E, 4G

Persuasive Writing

Writing Focus

- Persuasive Paragraph
- Persuasive Letter
- Across the Curriculum
- Assessment

Grammar Focus

- Subject-Verb Agreement
- Kinds of Sentences

Learning Language

Work with a partner. Read the meanings and share answers to the questions.

1. When you **persuade** someone, you get him or her to believe or act a certain way.
   When might you persuade someone?
2. A **community** is a group of people who live in the same place or do things together.
   What community are you a part of?
3. If something is **out of place**, it does not belong or is not in the correct location.
   Why is a fish out of place in the desert?

Healthy kids are happy kids! That is one child's opinion, or personal feeling. When you state an opinion, you let others know how you feel about a topic.

In persuasive writing, you try to get the reader to accept your opinion. If you are really persuasive, you may even be able to convince the reader to take action!

TEKS 2.20

Writing a
Persuasive
Paragraph

Eva's class was discussing healthy living. She noticed how tired her friend Polly looked. It gave her an idea for a persuasive paragraph. Eva decided to persuade her classmates to get more sleep.

In this chapter, you will write a paragraph to persuade your classmates, family, or local community to make a healthy choice.

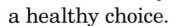

Eva's Persuasive Paragraph

Go to Sleep!

Topic Sentence

You should get ten hours of sleep each night. Sleep helps you stay healthy and happy. **Body Sentences** It gives your body and brain a rest from a hard day. Best of all, sleep gives you energy to do fun things, like jumping rope **Closing Sentence** and riding bikes. So every night, you should get plenty of sleep!

- The **topic sentence** states your opinion.
- The **body sentences** give two or three reasons for your opinion.
- The **closing sentence** tells the reader what action to take.

Prewriting ▶ Choosing Your Topic

To plan a persuasive paragraph, you first must generate ideas and select a strong topic.

This is what Eva did to find a topic for her paragraph. Eva thought about her class discussion. She then made a cluster of topic ideas and starred the strongest topic.

Topic Cluster

Prewrite ▶ **Choose your topic.**

1. Think about what you have learned about healthy living.
2. Make a cluster of topic ideas. Star the one you want to write about.

Prewriting ▶ Stating Your Opinion

You should then state your opinion or main feeling about your topic. This statement will be your topic sentence.

This is what Eva did to write her topic sentence. Eva thought about her feelings about her topic. Then she wrote her topic sentence by beginning with the words *you should*.

Topic Sentence

You should get ten hours of sleep each night.

Beginning with the words **you should** is a good way to start.

Prewrite ▶ **State your opinion.**

1. Think about the feelings you have about the topic you have chosen.
2. Write your topic sentence by beginning with the words *you should*.

Prewriting ▶ Gathering Details

Next, you should gather details to support your opinion.

This is what Eva did to gather details. She reviewed her topic sentence. Then Eva listed reasons for her opinion. She chose the most important reason and circled it.

Eva's Topic Sentence

You should get ten hours of sleep each night.

List of Reasons

Sleep helps you to be healthy and happy.

Sleep lets your body and brain rest.

⟨Sleep gives you more energy.⟩

Prewrite ▶ **Gather details.**

1. List the reasons for your opinion.
2. Choose the most important reason and circle it.

Drafting ▶ Writing Your First Draft

Your persuasive paragraph must contain a topic sentence, body sentences, and a closing sentence.

This is what Eva did to write the first draft of her persuasive paragraph. Eva reviewed her topic sentence (opinion statement) and reasons list. Then Eva wrote her paragraph. She followed these steps.

1. She started with her topic sentence or opinion statement.
2. Next, Eva stated her reasons in the body sentences.
3. She closed her paragraph by telling the reader to take action.

State your most important reason last.

Draft ▶ Write your first draft.

1. Review your opinion statement and reasons list.
2. Write your paragraph following Eva's three steps.

Revising ▶ Improving Your Writing

After finishing your first draft, it's time to improve your paragraph.

Eva revised her paragraph. First, she reviewed her opinion statement and three supporting reasons. Next, Eva checked that she had stated the most important reason last. Finally, she made any needed changes.

Be sure that you sound convincing in your paragraph.

Revise ▶ Improve your writing.

1. Review your opinion statement and reasons.
2. Check that your most important reason is last.
3. Add, take out, or change the order of ideas to improve your paragraph.

Editing ▶ Checking for Conventions

The next step is to check the conventions in your revised paragraph. (See page 452.)

This is what Eva did to edit her revised paragraph. First, she reviewed her paragraph for conventions using the checklist below. After checking, Eva corrected any errors.

Did you check?

✓ 1. Did you use correct verb tenses (present, past, and future)?

✓ 2. Did you capitalize names and the first word of each sentence?

✓ 3. Did you use punctuation at the end of each sentence?

✓ 4. Did you spell your words correctly?

Edit ▶ **Check for conventions.**

1. Review your revised paragraph for conventions. Use the checklist above as a guide.
2. Correct any errors that you find.

TEKS 2.20

Writing a
Persuasive Letter

"I eat too much junk food!" That was Mary's opinion about her diet. She wondered if she could do anything about it. She decided to write a persuasive letter to her mom and dad.

In this chapter, you will learn how to write a persuasive letter. In your letter, you will tell about one way to stay healthy.

 Understanding Your Goal

The traits below will help you write your letter. Read them carefully before you get started.

 **Focus** — Persuade someone to make a healthy living choice. Write about just one way to stay healthy.

Organization — Start with your opinion and follow it with supporting details.

 **Development of Ideas** — Support your opinion with details that are clear and interesting.

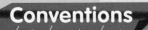 **Voice** — Sound serious and polite in your letter.

Conventions — Check for the parts of a letter, grammar, capitalization, punctuation, and spelling.

 Literature Connection: You can find a persuasive topic in *Raising Funds* by Ann Rossi.

TEKS 2.19B, 2.20

Mary's Persuasive Letter

Date ————— January 12, 2010

Salutation or Greeting ————— Dear Mom and Dad,

Body —————

We should remember to eat snacks that are healthy. At school, I tasted broccoli, yogurt, and soy nuts. Guess what? They taste good!

Vegetables, fruits, grains, and dairy foods are good for us. They can help us think, work, and play better. Best of all, they can keep us healthy.

I think we should eat many more healthy snacks. Please buy some extra ones the next time you go shopping.

Closing ————— Love,

Signature ————— Mary

Parts of a Letter

A friendly letter has five parts.

Date	The date tells when you wrote the letter.
Salutation or Greeting	The greeting is a polite way of saying, "Hi."
Body	The body is the main part of the letter.
Closing	The closing is a polite way of saying, "Good-bye."
Signature	The signature is the name of the writer at the end of the letter.

After You Read

1. **Organization** What closing does Mary use in her letter?
2. **Ideas** What is Mary's opinion? What does she want her parents to do?
3. **Voice** Do you think Mary was polite in her letter? Why or why not?

 TEKS 2.17A, 2.20

Prewriting ▶ Forming an Opinion

When planning to write a persuasive letter to someone in your school, home, or community, first form an opinion about a topic.

Here is what Conall did to get started.

Make   Conall generated ideas in a table diagram, and he starred the best topic.

Write   Next, Conall wrote his opinion statement about his topic.

Table Diagram

Staying Healthy

drink water	eat breakfast	* wash your hands

Write your own opinion statement by starting with **you should**.

You should **remember to wash your hands.**

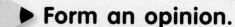

Prewrite ▶ Form an opinion.

1. Make a table diagram to list your topics.
2. Write an opinion statement about your topic.

Prewriting ▶ Gathering Details

Next, list reasons to support your opinion and decide who to write your letter to. You can write to someone in your school, home, or community.

Here's what Conall did to gather details.

List   He listed reasons to support his opinion and circled the most important one.

Pick   Then Conall decided to write to his mom and dad.

List of Reasons

Opinion:

You should remember to wash your hands.

Reasons:

To keep your food safe

To stop germs from spreading

To keep you from getting sick

 **Prewrite** ▶ **Gather details.**

1. List reasons to support your opinion and circle the most important one.

2. Pick someone in your school, home, or community to write to.

TEKS 2.17B, 2.19B, 2.20

Drafting ▶ Creating Your Letter

When you write your letter, be sure to include the five main parts. (See page 151.) Then concentrate on writing the body paragraphs.

This is what Conall did to write the body paragraphs for his persuasive letter.

I used these guidelines to write my first draft.

Guidelines

1. **Start** the **beginning paragraph** with your opinion. Then add one or two details about the topic.

2. **Explain** your reasons in the **middle paragraph.** Put your most important reason last.

3. In the **ending paragraph**, add an interesting detail and ask the reader to do something.

Conall's First Draft

March 18, 2011

Dear Mom and Dad,

Hi. You should remember to wash your hands. Germs live on your skin They even hide.

Wash your hands. It stops germs from spreading. Best of all, it keep you from getting sick. I don't like feeling sick. Keeps your food safer, too.

Come on! Make our home a healthyr place. Wash your hands!

Sincerely,

Conall

Draft ▶ Create your letter.

1. Write to someone in your school, home, or local community.
2. Follow the letter form on page 150.
3. Use the guidelines on page 154 to write your body paragraphs.

Revising for Focus

When you revise, you try to make your writing better. First, make sure all of your ideas are about your topic.

These are the things Conall did to revise his letter for focus.

Read   Conall read his first draft. He thought about the ideas in his letter.

Decide   Conall decided if each idea was about the importance of washing your hands.

Mark   He used the take out (✐) editing symbol to remove ideas that did not belong.

I took out the sentence that was not about washing your hands.

Conall's Revising

March 18, 2011

Dear Mom and Dad,

Hi. You should remember to wash your hands. Germs live on your skin They even hide.

Wash your hands. It stops germs from spreading. Best of all, it keep you from getting sick. ~~I don't like feeling sick.~~ Keeps your food safer, too.

Come on! Make our home a healthyr place. Wash your hands!

Sincerely,

Conall

Revise ▶ **Improve your focus.**

1. Review your first draft. Make sure all of your ideas are about your topic.
2. Mark the ideas you want to take out using the take out (_◯_) editing symbol.

Texas
Traits

Revising for **Organization**

When revising, pay careful attention to the order of your ideas. Move any of them that seem out of place.

Here's what Conall did to revise his body paragraphs for organization.

Review   Conall made sure that his opinion was stated in the beginning and that his supporting reasons were in the best order.

Ask   Conall asked his teacher to check his organization.

Reorder   He then moved any ideas that seemed out of place.

> I moved my most important reason last.

Conall's Revising

                                    March 18, 2011

Dear Mom and Dad,

        Hi. You should remember to wash
your hands. Germs live on your skin They
even hide.
        Wash your hands. It stops germs
from spreading. Best of all, it keep you
from getting sick. I don't like feeling sick.
Keeps your food safer, too.
        Come on! Make our home a healthyr
place. Wash your hands!

                                    Sincerely,
                                    Conall

Revise ▶ **Improve your organization.**

1. Review the first draft of your letter for
   organization and have a teacher read it, too.
2. Reorder any ideas that seem out of place.

TEKS 2.17C, 2.20
ELPS 3E, 5G

Revising for Development of Ideas

When you review your letter, pay careful attention to your ideas. Change any ideas that could be clearer or more interesting.

Here's what Conall did to revise his letter for ideas.

Review   Conall reviewed his letter to make sure that his details were clear and interesting.

Ask   He also asked a classmate to read his first draft.

Change   Conall then changed his writing to make it clearer.

I added two new details. It made my letter clearer and more interesting.

Conall's Revising

March 18, 2011

Dear Mom and Dad,

Hi. You should remember to wash your hands. Germs live on your skin They even hide.

~~scrub~~
with soap and water
∧Wash your hands∧. It stops germs from spreading. (Best of all, it keep you from getting sick.) ~~I don't like feeling sick.~~ Keeps your food safer, too.

Come on! Make our home a healthyr place. ∧Wash your hands!
Send those germs down the drain.

Sincerely,

Conall

Revise ▶ **Improve your ideas.**

1. Review the first draft of your letter and have a classmate read it, too.
2. Change any ideas that could be clearer.

TEKS 2.17C, 2.20
ELPS 1G, 3E, 5G

Revising for Voice

When revising, listen to the voice that you use. Change or cut any ideas that do not sound polite or serious enough for a persuasive letter.

Here's what Conall did to revise his letter for voice.

Read   First, Conall read his first draft to make sure that all of his ideas were polite and serious.

Listen   Then he listened while a classmate read the letter out loud.

Change   He changed or cut any ideas that did not have the right voice.

I cut two ideas that did not sound serious or polite enough.

Conall's Revising

March 18, 2011

Dear Mom and Dad,

⁹
Hi. You should remember to wash
your hands. Germs live on your skin They
even hide.
    scrub   with soap and water
    ᴧWash your hands. It stops germs
from spreading. Best of all, it keep you
from getting sick. i don't like feeling sick.
Keeps your food safer, too.⌄
        You can make
    ᴧCome on! Make our home a healthyr
Send those germs down the drain.
place.ᴧWash your hands!

Sincerely,
Conall

Revise ▶ Improve your voice.

1. Read your first draft and listen while
   a classmate reads it out loud to you.
2. Change or cut any ideas as needed.

TEKS 2.21B
ELPS 2C, 2I, 3G, 3E, 5D

Editing for Conventions

Grammar

When you edit for grammar, you make sure you use words correctly.

How do I write a complete sentence?

A **complete sentence** has a **subject** and a **predicate**. The subject is who or what the sentence is about. The predicate tells what the subject does.

Micah's cat eats corn on the cob.

The **predicate** always includes a **verb**, or action word. The verb must agree with the subject of the sentence. This is called **subject-verb agreement**.

Correct: Kim plays kickball.
Incorrect: Kim play kickball.

Grammar practice

Talk It Over Tell a partner which part is missing in each sentence below. Then complete each sentence and write it on a piece of paper.

1. A flower _____.
2. _____ like cheese.
3. _____ has a bike.
4. Students _____.
5. Our school _____.
6. _____ can do tricks.

What are some kinds of sentences?

Telling sentences make a statement or tell a fact. They end with a period.

Sara eats cereal for breakfast.

My favorite sport is soccer.

Asking sentences ask a question. They end with a question mark.

What is your favorite holiday?

Did you like the book?

Grammar Practice

Talk It Over Rewrite each sentence using the correct end punctuation. Explain to a partner why you chose a period or a question mark.

1. Your sister is friendly
2. Was the car yellow
3. The Estebans enjoyed their trip
4. What will you do after school
5. What is your favorite food

Learning Language

Take turns asking and answering questions. Ask your partner a question about a favorite food, sport, or activity. Your partner should answer with a complete sentence. Then switch roles.

TEKS 2.19B, 2.20, 2.21B, 2.22B(i), 2.22C(i)
ELPS 1B, 5C, 5D

Texas
Traits
Editing for Conventions

When you edit, you check your writing for conventions. (See page 452.)

This is how Conall edited his letter.

Review Conall reviewed his letter to make sure it included the five main parts. (See page 151.)

Check He also checked his letter for any errors. He used the rubric on pages 168–169 as a guide.

Correct Then Conall marked his errors and corrected them.

I used editing marks to fix my errors.

Did you check?

✔ 1. Did you use complete sentences with subject-verb agreement?

✔ 2. Did you use correct capitalization and punctuation?

✔ 3. Did you spell your words correctly?

Conall's Editing

March 18, 2011

Dear Mom and Dad,

You should remember to wash your hands. Germs live on your skin. They even hide.

S

scrub your hands with soap and water. It stops germs from spreading.

Washing hands

Keeps your food safer, too. Best of all, it

keeps

~~keep~~ you from getting sick.

healthier

You can make our home a ~~healthyr~~ place. Send those germs down the drain. Wash your hands!

Sincerely,

Conall

Edit ▶ **Check for conventions.**

1. Check your letter for grammar, capitalization, punctuation, and spelling. Use the rubric.
2. Check, mark, and correct any errors.

 TEKS 2.17D, 2.19B, 2.20, 2.21B, 2.21C, 2.22B(ii), 2.22B(iii), 2.22C(i)
ELPS 1B, 4K, 5C, 5D

 Texas Traits

Editing Using a Rubric

Use this rubric while you edit to improve your writing. Remember when you edit, you make sure that you have followed the rules for grammar, capitalization, punctuation, and spelling.

4 In my writing:

- All of my sentences are complete sentences with subject-verb agreement.

- I used the correct end punctuation (. ? !) for all sentences.

- I started all sentences with capital letters.

- I included all parts of a letter.

- I capitalized all of these letter parts: date, salutation, and closing.

- I spelled all words correctly.

3 In my writing:

- Most of my sentences are complete sentences with subject-verb agreement.

- I used the correct end punctuation (. ? !) for most sentences.

- I started most sentences with capital letters.

- I included most parts of a letter.

- I capitalized two of these letter parts: date, salutation, and closing.

- I spelled most words correctly.

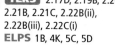

Using a rubric helps me make my writing better!

 In my writing:

- Some of my sentences are complete sentences with subject-verb agreement.

- I used the correct end punctuation (. ? !) for some sentences.

- I started some sentences with capital letters.

- I included some parts of a letter.

- I capitalized one of these letter parts: date, salutation, and closing.

- I spelled some words correctly.

 In my writing:

- None of my sentences are complete sentences with subject-verb agreement.

- I did not use the correct end punctuation (. ? !) for any sentences.

- I did not start any sentences with capital letters.

- I did not include any parts of a letter.

- I did not capitalize any letter parts.

- I misspelled many words.

TEKS 2.17E, 2.20
ELPS 2I, 3E

Publishing ▶ **Sharing Your Letter**

When you publish your writing, you share the final copy. There are many different ways to publish. (See page 33.)

Here's what Conall did to publish his letter.

Write   Conall wrote a neat final copy of his letter. He included all of his revising and editing changes.

Read   Then he read this copy to be sure it was neat and free of mistakes.

I shared my letter and then added it to my writing portfolio.

Conall's Persuasive Letter

> March 18, 2011
>
> Dear Mom and Dad,
>
>   You should remember to wash your hands. Germs live on your skin. They even hide.
>   Scrub your hands with soap and water. It stops germs from spreading. Washing hands keeps your food safer, too. Best of all, it keeps you from getting sick.
>   You can make our home a healthier place. Send those germs down the drain. Wash your hands!
>
>   Sincerely,
>   Conall

Publish ▶ **Share your letter.**

1. Write a neat copy of your letter.
2. Read the final copy before you share it.

TEKS 2.17E

Sending Your Letter

To send your letter, fold it neatly into three parts. Then put it into an envelope.

> Remember: The U.S. Postal Service asks that you use all capital letters and no punctuation when addressing your envelope.

Addressing Your Envelope

1. Write your name and address in the upper left corner.
2. In the middle of the envelope, write the name and address of the person who will get your letter.
3. Place a stamp in the upper right corner.

CONALL RIOS
3421 FOREST LANE
DALLAS TX 75234

USA ¢

MR AND MRS RIOS
3421 FOREST LANE
DALLAS TX 75234

Reflecting on Your Writing

Take a few minutes to think about your writing. Complete the two sentences below.

Thinking About Your Writing

Name: _Conall Rios_

Title: _Persuasive Letter_

1. The best thing about my letter is

   the part about sending germs

   right down the drain!

2. The main thing I learned while writing

   my letter is _that it's important to_

   have good reasons for your opinion.

Writing
Across the Curriculum
Science: Endangered Animal Paragraph

For science, Juanita wrote a persuasive paragraph about an endangered animal.

Save the Tigers

Topic Sentence

Our class should help save the tigers.
We could have a penny drive and give
the pennies to the Wild Tiger Fund. Then

Body Sentences

people could use the money to save the
grasslands where tigers live. We need to
take action. It would be sad to see
these big, beautiful cats disappear.
The tigers really need us. Please say yes

Closing Sentence

to a penny drive!

Writing Tips

Use these tips to write your
own persuasive paragraph.

Cluster

Before You Write

> **Think** of a cause that you
> have discussed in class.
>
> **Form** an opinion statement
> about one of these causes.
>
> **Use** a cluster to gather
> supporting reasons.

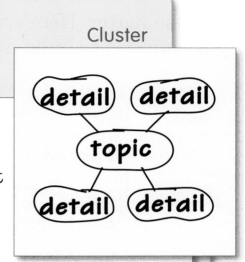

During Your Writing

> **State** your opinion in the topic sentence.
>
> **Give** reasons for supporting this cause
> in the body sentences.
>
> **Ask** your reader to take action in the
> closing sentence.

After You Have Written

> **Be sure** you included important reasons.
>
> **Check** your grammar, capitalization,
> punctuation, and spelling.

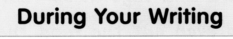

⭐ TEKS 2.19B, 2.20

Social Studies: A Letter to the Mayor

For social studies, Henry wrote a letter to the mayor. Henry asked the mayor for permission to build a community garden.

Date

Salutation or Greeting

Body Sentences

Closing

Signature

February 3, 2011

Dear Mrs. Martinson,

    Our class would like to build a community garden in the old parking lot downtown. People could plant flowers and vegetables there. They could even eat the food they grow!

    A community garden would make the downtown area more beautiful and more fun. I think it is a great way to make our city better. I hope you agree! Please give us permission to build our community garden.

Sincerely,

Henry Torres

Writing Tips

Use these tips to write your own persuasive letter.

Before You Write

Think of something in your community that you would like to change.

Answer the 5 W questions.

Choose a community leader to write your letter to.

5 W's Chart

Who?	
What?	
When?	
Where?	
Why?	

During Your Writing

Begin with the date and the salutation.

Give your opinion and reasons in an order that makes sense.

Close with *Sincerely,* and sign your full name.

After You Have Written

Be sure your letter is clear and polite.

Correct any errors in conventions and make a neat final copy.

Send your letter!

Writing for Assessment

You may be asked to write a persuasive paragraph for a writing assessment.

Writing Prompt

Imagine that your class can take a field trip to any place you have studied. Choose a place. In one paragraph, persuade your class to go there.

Think   Lila thought about places to go.

Choose   She chose to write about a very special place, Washington, D.C.

List   Then she listed reasons to support her choice. She circled the most important reason.

List of Reasons

1. We could go to the White House.
2. We might meet the president.
3. We could visit the National Zoo.

Lila's Persuasive Paragraph

A Capital Idea

The **topic sentence** names the place.	Our class should go to Washington, D.C. **It is an exciting city with many things to see and do. First, we'll visit the National**
The **body sentences** explain the field trip.	**Zoo. Next, we could see the White House where many presidents have lived. Best of all, we might even**
The **closing sentences** give a call to action.	**meet the president.** We should plan a field trip to Washington, D.C. Let's do it!

practice

1. Choose a place you have studied.
2. List reasons like the ones on page 178.
3. Write your persuasive paragraph.

Literature Connection: You can find a persuasive topic in *Ready for Liftoff* by Ann Takman.

ELPS 2C, 2G, 2I, 3E, 4G

Response to Texts

Writing Focus

- Response Paragraph
- Reviewing a Fiction Book
- Reviewing a Nonfiction Book
- Comparing Fiction Books
- Responding to a Poem
- Assessment

Learning Language

Work with a partner. Read the meanings and share answers to the questions.

1. When you read **literature**, you read stories, books, or poems.
   What kinds of literature do you like?

2. When you **compare**, you decide how two things are alike.
   Compare yourself and your partner.

3. If you **give away** a surprise, you tell about it before you should.
   Why shouldn't you give away the ending of a book or movie?

Don't keep a good book to yourself. Tell your friends about it! Talking about books can be fun. You can also share your ideas by writing about the books you've read.

In this section, you will learn how to write about literature and informational texts. Writing about the stories and poems that you read really helps you think about them—and understand them better.

Writing a
Response
Paragraph

After Mark read a story, he decided he was like one of the characters. He wrote about this idea in a response paragraph.

In this chapter, you will respond to a story in the same way.

Mark's Response Paragraph

By Myself

Topic Sentence

I am like Frog in the book <u>Days with Frog and Toad</u> by Arnold Lobel. In the story, Frog writes Toad a note. It says, "I went out, and I want to be alone." Toad

Body Sentences

thinks Frog does not want to be his friend, but Frog just wants to be by himself. Sometimes I like to be alone, too. Maybe I will write

Closing Sentence

my friends a note like that. I hope they will understand how I feel.

- The **topic sentence** names the character, the book, and the author.
- The **body sentences** tell how the writer is like the character.
- The **closing sentence** shares one last idea.

TEKS 2.17A, 2.19C
ELPS 4G, 4K

Prewriting ▶ Gathering Details

After you select a story to write about, gather details for your response paragraph.

Mark finished the sentence starters below to gather details about the story he read.

Sentence Starters

1. The title of this book is _Days with Frog and Toad_

2. The author is _Arnold Lobel_

3. I am like _Frog_ because _sometimes I like to be alone._

4. The part of the story that shows this is _when Frog writes to Toad._

Prewrite ▶ Gather your details.

1. Choose a book you would like to write about.
2. Then finish the sentence starters above on your own paper.

Drafting ▶ **Writing Your First Draft**

Use the details you have gathered to write your paragraph. Include a topic sentence, body sentences, and a closing sentence.

> Mark wrote his first draft using ideas from the sentence starters on page 184.

Draft ▶ **Write your paragraph.**

1. Write your topic sentence.

I am like _____ *(character's name)*
in the book _____ *(book's title)*
by _____ *(name of author)* .

2. Write body sentences. Show how you are like the character. Use one example from the story.
3. End with a closing sentence. Share one last idea about your topic.

TEKS 2.17C
ELPS 1B, 5G

Revising ▶ Improving Your Writing

Review your first draft to make sure the ideas are clear and easy to follow. Then change any parts as needed.

Mark carefully reviewed his first draft using the checklist below as a guide. Then he changed parts that could be improved.

Did you review?

✓ 1. Did you name the book and author?

✓ 2. Did you tell how you are like one of the characters?

✓ 3. Did you use an example from the story to show this?

✓ 4. Did you put your ideas in order so they make sense?

Revise ▶ Improve your writing.

1. Review your first draft using the checklist above as a guide.

2. Add, take out, or change parts to improve your paragraph.

Editing ▶ Checking Your Conventions

When you edit your paragraph, you check it for conventions. (See page 452.) It's important that you use correct grammar, capitalization, punctuation, and spelling.

Mark edited his writing using the checklist as a guide. He also asked a classmate to check his writing.

Did you check?

✔ 1. Did you indent the first line of your paragraph?

✔ 2. Did you underline the book's title?

✔ 3. Did you use complete sentences?

✔ 4. Did you capitalize names and the first word in each sentence?

✔ 5. Did you use a punctuation mark after each sentence?

✔ 6. Did you check your spelling?

Edit ▶ **Check for conventions.**

1. Edit your writing for conventions using the checklist above as a guide.
2. Also ask a classmate to check your paragraph.

Reviewing a
Fiction Book

A fiction (make-believe) book helps you imagine another world. Stacy, who lives in a big city, enjoyed reading *All the Places to Love*. The book helped her imagine living in the country. She wrote a review about the story.

In this chapter, you will write a review about a fiction book you have read.

Stacy's Book Review

Special Places

Beginning

All the Places to Love was written by Patricia MacLachlan. In the story, a boy named Eli lives on a farm. He wants to share his special places with his new baby sister.

Middle

My favorite part is when Baby Sylvie is born. Eli thinks about showing her the marsh. It is his favorite place. A turtle lives there, and baby ducklings swim in the water.

Ending

You should read this book. The words sound like a poem, and the pictures are pretty. If you live in the city, Eli will share his farm with you.

After You Read

1. **Organization** What does the middle part of the review tell about?

2. **Ideas** What is the main idea of the book?

Prewriting ▶ Selecting a Topic

To get started, think of your favorite fiction books. Then choose one to be the topic of your review.

Here's how Zola selected a book for her review.

Build Zola built a question grid about her two favorite fiction books and circled one book to review.

Question Grid

What is the title?	Who is the author?	Why do I like the book?
Cloudy with a Chance of Meatballs	Judi Barrett	It is very funny.
Nate the Great	Marjorie Weinman Sharmat and Mitchell Sharmat	I like mysteries.

Prewrite ▶ **Select a topic.**

1. Fill in a question grid about your two favorite books.
2. Circle the book you want to write about.

Prewriting ▶ Gathering Details

After selecting a favorite book, you need to gather details before you can write about it.

Here's what Zola did to gather details for her book review.

Fill in   Zola filled in a 5 W's chart with important details from the book.

5 W's Chart

Who?	Nate, his dog Sludge, and Duncan were there.
What?	Duncan lost his joke book. Nate helped him find it.
When?	The story happened yesterday.
Where?	The story happened in San Francisco.
Why?	Duncan made a mess at the Pancake House.

Prewrite ▶ **Gather details.**

Fill in a 5 W's chart like the one above about your book.

TEKS 2.17B
ELPS 4G, 5G

Drafting ▶ Beginning Your Review

In your beginning paragraph, name the book and the author. Also tell what the book is about.

This is how Zola began.

Beginning

Middle

Ending

Write Zola checked her 5 W's chart for details and wrote her beginning paragraph.

Zola's Beginning Paragraph

Nate the Great, San Francisco Detective was written by Marjorie Weinman Sharmat and Mitchell Sharmat. In this story, Nate goes to San Francisco. He helps a boy named Duncan look for a lost book. Nate is a great detective because he finds lots of clues.

Draft ▶ Begin your review.

Write your beginning using your 5 W's chart.

Drafting ▶ Telling Just Enough

In Zola's beginning paragraph, she did not give away any of the surprises or the story's ending. She told just enough details to make her friends want to read the book for themselves.

Practice

Here is another beginning paragraph about Zola's book. Which two sentences give away surprises? Tell why these sentences should be left out.

(1) Nate the Great, San Francisco Detective was written by Marjorie Weinman Sharmat and Mitchell Sharmat. (2) The story happens in San Francisco. (3) Nate, the detective, helps a boy named Duncan look for a lost book. (4) It is in the bookstore on the wrong shelf. (5) In the end, the mystery is solved.

Drafting ▶ Developing the Middle

The middle paragraph of your review should tell about your favorite part of the book.

Here's what Zola did to write the middle paragraph of her review.

Beginning

▶ Middle

Ending

Think Zola thought about her favorite part of the book.

Write Then she wrote a paragraph about this part. She shared the details in time order.

Zola's Middle Paragraph

> The best part is when Nate digs for clues in a messy bag. He finds dirty napkins, cold pancakes, and a small tub of butter. It gets worse. Sticky maple syrup is on everything!

Draft ▶ **Develop the middle.**

Write a paragraph about your favorite part of the book.

Drafting ▶ Completing the Ending

The ending paragraph of your review should tell why you think other readers will enjoy the book.

Here's how Zola wrote her ending.

	Beginning
	Middle
	▶ Ending

Think   Zola thought about why she liked the book.

Decide   She decided her classmates would like it for the same reason.

Write   Then Zola wrote her ending paragraph.

Zola's Ending Paragraph

> **Do you wish you were a detective? You can be one when you read** <u>Nate the Great, San Francisco Detective</u>**. It is fun trying to solve the mystery. See if you can figure it out before Nate does.**

Draft ▶ Complete the ending.

Write your ending paragraph. Tell why your classmates should read the book.

TEKS 2.17C
ELPS 1B, 5G

Revising ▶ Improving Your Writing

You should review your first draft and revise or change any ideas that could be clearer.

Here's what Zola did to revise her first draft.

Review   Zola reviewed her writing using the checklist below as a guide.

Identify   She identified any parts that could be clearer.

Change   Then Zola changed the parts that needed work.

Did you review?

✓ 1. Did you name the book and its author?

✓ 2. Did you share your favorite part?

✓ 3. Did you include just enough details without spoiling the ending?

Revise ▶ **Improve your writing.**

1. Review your first draft using the checklist above.
2. Change any parts that need work.

Editing ▶ Checking for Conventions

After revising your book review, you should check it for grammar, capitalization, punctuation, and spelling. (See page 452.)

This is what Zola did to edit her writing.

Use   Zola used the questions below as an editing guide.

Mark   She marked any convention errors.

Correct   Then Zola corrected the errors.

Did you check?

✓ 1. Did you use complete sentences?

✓ 2. Did you capitalize names and the first word in each sentence?

✓ 3. Did you use correct punctuation (. ? !) after each sentence?

✓ 4. Did you underline the book's title?

✓ 5. Did you check your spelling?

Edit ▶ **Check for conventions.**

Edit your writing using the checklist above.

Publishing ▸ Sharing Your Review

Zola's Book Review

The Great Nate

    <u>Nate the Great, San Francisco Detective</u> was written by Marjorie Weinman Sharmat and Mitchell Sharmat. In this story, Nate goes to San Francisco. He helps a boy named Duncan look for a lost book. Nate is a great detective because he finds lots of clues.

    The best part is when Nate digs for clues in a messy bag. He finds dirty napkins, cold pancakes, and a small tub of butter. It gets worse. Sticky maple syrup is on everything!

    Do you wish you were a detective? You can be one when you read <u>Nate the Great, San Francisco Detective</u>. It is fun trying to solve the mystery. See if you can figure it out before Nate does.

Publish ▸ **Share a neat final copy of your review.**

Reflecting on Your Writing

After you finish your review, take some time to think about it. Then fill in a sheet like this about your review.

Thinking About Your Writing

Name: _Zola_

Title: _The Great Nate_

1. The best part about my review is

   the ending. My question makes

   the reader think.

2. The main thing I learned while writing

   my review is _that it's really important_

   not to give the whole story away.

Reviewing a
Nonfiction Book

Nonfiction books give true facts about real people, places, and things. Lee wrote a review about the nonfiction book *Cactus Hotel*. Read his review and then learn how to write one of your own.

Lee's Book Review

A Desert Home

Beginning

Cactus Hotel is a book by Brenda Z. Guiberson. It tells about the life of a saguaro cactus. This giant plant grows in the desert.

Middle

Here are some interesting facts from the book. When it rains, a saguaro cactus gets fat. A saguaro can live for 200 years. Birds make holes in the cactus. The holes become homes for animals.

Ending

My favorite page shows birds, bugs, and rats living inside a saguaro cactus. When one animal moves out, another one moves in. Can you see why it is called a cactus hotel?

After You Read

1. **Organization** What does the ending part tell about?
2. **Ideas** What is the main idea of the book?

Prewriting ▶ Selecting a Topic

To get started, think of your favorite nonfiction books. Then choose one to be the topic of your review.

Here's what Debra did to select a book.

Make Debra made a chart about two of her favorite nonfiction books. (See below.)

Star Then Debra starred the book she chose.

Book Chart

Title 1	Jambo Means Hello *
Author	Muriel Feelings
Main Idea	Swahili words tell about life in Africa.
Title 2	All Pigs Are Beautiful
Author	Dick King-Smith
Main Idea	You learn all about pigs.

Prewrite ▶ Select a topic.

1. Make a book chart about two favorite nonfiction books.
2. Star the book that you want to review.

Prewriting ▶ Gathering Details

After you choose a nonfiction book, gather details about it for your review.

This is what Debra did to gather details.

Answer   Debra answered three important questions about the book. (See below.)

Question and Answer Sheet

What is the book about?
—life in Africa.
—Swahili words for each alphabet letter
What facts do I think are most interesting?
—school is outdoors
—Watoto, the Swahili word for children
—children tending cattle and hauling water
Which is my favorite part and why?
—Children dancing and playing looks like fun!

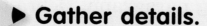 **Prewrite** ▶ **Gather details.**

To gather details, answer the three questions above about your book.

Drafting ▶ Your First Draft

Your review should include three parts: the beginning paragraph, the middle paragraph, and the ending paragraph. Each paragraph will answer one of the questions that you answered on page 203.

This is what Debra did to write her first draft.

Review   Debra reviewed her answers to the questions on page 203.

Write   Then she wrote her first draft.

In the **beginning** paragraph, Debra named the book's title and author. She also told what the book is about.

She shared at least three interesting facts in the **middle** paragraph.

In the **ending** paragraph, Debra told about her favorite part.

Beginning

> Jambo Means Hello is a book by Muriel Feelings. It is about life in Africa. The book shows one Swahili word for each letter of the alphabet. Swahili is one of Africa's languages.

Middle

> Here are some interesting facts in the book. Kids in Africa go to school outside. They have many hard chores to do. They take care of the cattle. They also haul water from the river. The Swahili word for children is Watoto.

Ending

> My favorite part shows kids dancing and playing. The book says that they sing funny songs and dance with quick steps. I wish I could play with them.

Draft ▶ **Write your first draft.**

1. Review your answers to the questions on page 203.
2. Write your first draft using the sample above as a guide.

 **TEKS** 2.17C
ELPS 1B, 5G

Revising ▶ Improving Your Writing

Revise or change any ideas in your writing that could be clearer.

This is what Debra did to revise her writing.

Study Debra studied her first draft using the checklist below as a guide.

Change Then she changed any parts that could be clearer or more complete.

Did you review?

✔ 1. Did you name the book and its author?
✔ 2. Did you tell what the book is about?
✔ 3. Did you share at least three important facts?
✔ 4. Did you tell about your favorite part?
✔ 5. Are your ideas clear?

Revise ▶ **Improve your writing.**

1. Study your first draft using the checklist above as a guide.
2. Change any parts that could be clearer or more complete.

Editing ▶ Checking for Conventions

After revising your book review, you should check it for grammar, capitalization, punctuation, and spelling. (See page 452.) Ask a classmate to help, too.

Here's what Debra did to edit her review.

Check Debra edited her writing using the questions below as a guide.

Mark She marked any convention errors.

Correct Then Debra corrected the errors.

Did you check?

✓ 1. Did you use correct subject-verb agreement?

✓ 2. Did you capitalize names and the first word in each sentence?

✓ 3. Did you use correct punctuation (. ? !) after each sentence?

✓ 4. Did you underline the book's title?

✓ 5. Did you check your spelling?

Edit ▶ **Check for conventions.**

Edit your writing using the checklist above.

TEKS 2.17E
ELPS 2I, 3E

Publishing ▶ Sharing Your Review

Debra's Book Review

Jambo!

    <u>Jambo Means Hello</u> is a book by Muriel Feelings. It is about life in Africa. The book shows one Swahili word for each letter of the alphabet. Swahili is one of Africa's languages.

    Here are some interesting facts in the book. Kids in Africa go to school outside. They have many hard chores to do. They take care of the cattle. They also haul water from the river. The Swahili word for children is Watoto.

    My favorite page shows kids dancing and playing. The book says that they sing funny songs and dance with quick steps. I wish I could play with them.

Publish ▶ **Share a neat final copy of your review.**

Reflecting on Your Writing

After you finish your review, take some time to think about it. Then fill in a sheet like this about your review.

Thinking About Your Writing

Name: _Debra_

Title: _Jambo!_

1. The best part about my review is

   the middle. The facts are

   interesting.

2. The main thing I learned while writing

   my review is _how to tell what the book_

   is about in two or three sentences.

Comparing
Fiction Books

Do you have a favorite author? Travis really likes Tomie dePaola. He read two great books by this author. Then he compared the two books in an essay. Read his comparison and learn how to write one of your own.

Travis's Comparison Essay

Two Long Ago Stories

Beginning   My favorite author is Tomie dePaola. I read his books <u>The Legend of the Indian Paintbrush</u> and <u>Jamie O'Rourke and the Big Potato</u>.

Middle   The books are alike because they take place long ago. Both stories are about plants. The books are different, too. In one story, the plant is a potato. In the other, it is an Indian Paintbrush. One story takes place in Ireland, and the other happens in America.

Ending   I like <u>Jamie O'Rourke and the Big Potato</u> best because it is funny. I like funny stories.

After You Read

1. **Organization** What information does the beginning give?
2. **Ideas** How are the two books different?

Prewriting ▶ Selecting a Topic

Think of two books by one of your favorite authors to compare. Or think of one book that you really like and find another book by the same author.

Here's what Kamika did to select two books to compare.

Name Kamika named one of her favorite authors, Jan Brett.

Choose Then she chose two books by this author to compare: Hedgie's Surprise and Daisy Comes Home.

You may have to use the computer in your library to find one of your books.

Prewrite ▶ **Select a topic.**

1. Name your favorite author.
2. Choose two books by that author to compare. (Or think of your favorite book and another book by the same author.)

Prewriting ▶ Gathering Details

Use a graphic organizer like a Venn diagram to gather details for your comparison essay.

This is what Kamika did to gather details.

Fill in Kamika filled in a Venn diagram with details about how the books are alike and different.

Venn Diagram

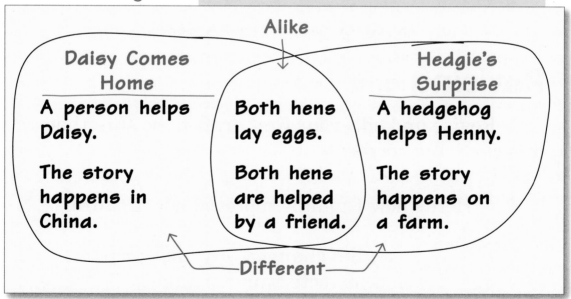

Alike

Daisy Comes Home	Both hens lay eggs.	Hedgie's Surprise
A person helps Daisy.		A hedgehog helps Henny.
The story happens in China.	Both hens are helped by a friend.	The story happens on a farm.

Different

Prewrite ▶ **Gather details.**

Fill in a Venn diagram to show how your books are alike and different.

 TEKS 2.17B, 2.17C

Drafting ▶ Writing Your First Draft

Write the beginning, middle, and ending parts of your comparison essay.

> Here's how Kamika wrote her first draft.
>
> **Develop**   Kamika used page 211 and her Venn diagram to develop her essay.

Draft ▶ **Write your first draft.**

Develop the three parts of your essay.

Revising and Editing

Revise and edit your first draft to be sure that it is clear and correct.

> Here's how Kamika improved her first draft.
>
> **Change**   Kamika changed any unclear parts and corrected any mistakes.

Revise ▶ **and** **Edit** ▶

Change your essay to make it clear and correct.

Publishing ▶ Sharing Your Comparison

Kamika's Comparison Essay

Two Hens

    I read two books by Jan Brett. They are
<u>Daisy Comes Home</u> and <u>Hedgie's Surprise</u>.
    The books are alike because they are
about hens that lay eggs. Both hens get help
from a friend. The books are different, too.
One hen is named Henny, and she lives on a
farm. A hedgehog named Hedgie helps Henny.
The other hen is named Daisy. She lives in
a sandy yard in China. Daisy's helper is a
person named Mei Mei.
    I liked <u>Daisy Comes Home</u> best because
the setting is China. The pictures show an
interesting, faraway place.

Publish ▶ **Share a neat final copy of
your comparison.**

Responding to a
Poem

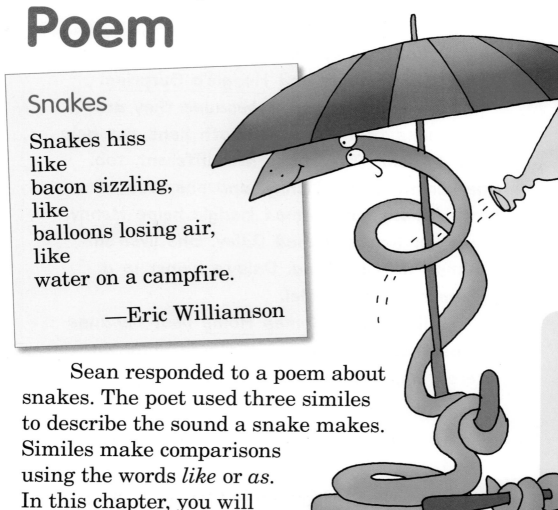

Snakes

Snakes hiss
like
bacon sizzling,
like
balloons losing air,
like
water on a campfire.

—Eric Williamson

Sean responded to a poem about snakes. The poet used three similes to describe the sound a snake makes. Similes make comparisons using the words *like* or *as*. In this chapter, you will learn how to respond to a simile poem.

Sean's Response Essay

Sizzling Snakes

Beginning

    "Snakes" is a poem about sounds. It compares a snake's hissing to other sounds.

Middle

    My favorite simile is "Snakes hiss like bacon sizzling." I've heard bacon sizzling on the stove. Ssss! That's a hiss I love to hear.

Ending

    I think the poet wrote this poem because he likes using words creatively. His hissing similes are fun to read.

After You Read

1. **Organization** What does the ending part tell about?
2. **Ideas** What is the writer's favorite simile? Why does he like it?

Prewriting ▶ Choosing a Poem

Read the simile poems on this page. Think about which one you'd like to write about.

Thunder

Thunder rumbles
like
a space shuttle launch,
like
a big bass drum,
like
fireworks!

—Darin Hall

Let's Fly!

Birds fly
like
paper airplanes,
like
leaves in the winds,
like
sparks from a fire.

—Sue Ling

Stars

Stars sparkle
like
Grandfather's eyes,
like
Mother's earrings,
like
my shiny blue shoes.

—Jenna Matson

Leap Frog

Frogs leap
like
funny clowns,
like
kangaroos,
like
tummies on a
    roller coaster!

—Ty Petski

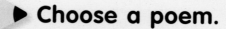

Prewrite ▶ **Choose a poem.**

Prewriting ▶ Gathering Details

The next step is to gather details in the poem for your response.

Here's what Mandy did to gather details.

Complete Mandy completed the sentence starters below to gather her details.

> **Spring**
>
> Flower buds wait
> like
> wrapped presents,
> like
> chicks inside eggs,
> like
> pages in a book.
>
> —Ellie Taylor

Sentence Starters

1. The poem " <u>Spring</u> " is about <u>flower buds</u> .

2. My favorite simile is " <u>Flower buds wait</u> <u>like pages in a book</u> ."

3. I think the poet wrote the poem because <u>she likes spring</u> .

Prewrite  ▶ **Gather details.**

Copy and complete the sentence starters above.

Drafting ▶ Writing Your First Draft

Develop the beginning, middle, and ending parts of your response.

> This is how Mandy wrote her response.
>
> **Develop** Mandy developed the three parts of her response using page 217 and her sentence starters as a guide.

Draft ▶ **Write your first draft.**

Develop your first draft.

Revising and Editing

Be sure that your ideas are clear and correct.

> Here's how Mandy improved her response.
>
> **Change** Mandy changed any unclear parts and corrected any mistakes.

Revise ▶ and **Edit** ▶

Change your essay to make it clear and correct.

Publishing ▶ Sharing Your Response

Mandy's Response Essay

> ### A Long Wait
>
>   "Spring" is a poem about flower buds.
> The buds are waiting to open. It is the
> season of spring.
>   My favorite simile is "Flower buds wait
> like pages in a book." I thought about that
> for a long time. With a book, spring can come
> at any time of the year. Pages in a book are
> always waiting for somebody to read them.
>   Maybe the poet wrote this poem
> because she is waiting for spring. She might
> have a flower garden in her backyard.

Publish ▶ **Make a neat final copy to share.**

TEKS 2.17A, 2.19C
ELPS 5G

Writing for Assessment

On most writing tests, you will read a prompt and write a paragraph about it.

Writing Prompt

Pretend you are one of the characters in your favorite story. Write a paragraph that tells who you are, what is happening, and how you feel.

Think   Terri thought about her favorite story.

Choose   She chose a character and a part of the story to write about.

Fill in   Then she filled in a 5 W's chart to gather details.

Literature Connection: You can read Terri's favorite story in *The Tale of Ginger and Pickles* by Beatrix Potter.

Terri's Chart and Response

Who?	Pickles the dog
What?	worried about my dog license
When?	January 1
Where?	in the store
Why?	because we have no money

My name is Pickles, and I run a store with Ginger the cat. I am worried because we have no money at our store, and I can't pay for my dog license. I will ask our customers to pay their bills.

practice

1. Choose a character from your favorite story.
2. Use a 5 W's chart to gather details. Then write a response paragraph.

ELPS 2C, 2I, 3E, 4G

Creative Writing

Writing Focus

- Add-On Stories
- Plays
- Poems

Learning Language

Work with a partner. Read the meanings and share your answers.

1. A **character** is a person in a story or play. Animals or objects can also be **characters**.
   Who are the characters in your favorite story?

2. **Stage directions** tell actors what to do.
   Why are stage directions important?

3. A **storyboard** is a set of pictures that show the parts of a story in order.
   Draw a storyboard that shows what you have done today.

4. When you **set up** something, you put its parts together and get it ready.
   How would you set up a board game?

This is what author Clyde Robert Bulla thinks about words and writing: "Words are wonderful. By writing them and putting them together, I could make them say whatever I wanted to say. It was a kind of magic."

In this section, you will put words together in special ways in your own stories, plays, and poems. So, get ready . . . get set . . . imagine!

226

Writing
Add-On Stories

You can use your imagination by writing add-on stories. In Angela's add-on story, the main character has a problem. One by one, new characters are added to the story. In the end, something surprising happens, and the problem is solved.

Parts of a Story

Every story has four special parts: characters, setting, problem, and plot.

Characters The characters are the people or animals in your story.

Setting The setting tells the time and place of your story.

Problem The problem is the trouble the characters face in the story.

Plot The plot is the action in the story.

Angela's Add-On Story

Go Away, Clouds

Sun had a problem. She was shining, but no one could see her. Clouds were in the way.

Wind tried to help. He huffed and puffed. The clouds wouldn't move.

Then Moon came along. He said, "Go to sleep, Sun. When you wake, the clouds will be gone." The Moon glowed all night. The clouds wouldn't move.

Finally, Wolf came along and howled at Moon. "Owoooo!" Suddenly, the clouds got scared and flew away.

In the morning, the clouds were gone. Sun felt happy because everyone could see her now.

After You Read

Ideas What are the four parts of the story?
Who are the add-on characters?

 **TEKS** 2.17A
ELPS 3E, 3G

Prewriting ▶ Selecting Your Topic

To get started, you need to think of a main character, a problem, and a setting for your add-on story. All stories *start* with these three parts.

Here's what Hunter did to start his add-on story.

Talk Hunter talked with a classmate about his story ideas. She asked him about his characters and what kinds of problems they could have.

Build Then Hunter built a story questions chart, naming the main parts for his story. The chart answered the who, what, when, and where of his story.

Will your main character be a person, an animal, or an object like the sun?

Hunter's Story Questions Chart

Who is the main character?	rabbit
What problem happens?	stuck in a hole
When does the story happen?	morning
Where does the story happen?	outside

Prewrite ▶ **Select your topic.**

1. Talk about your story ideas with a partner.
2. Build a story questions chart that answers the who, what, when, and where of your story.

Prewriting ► Gathering Details

Once you complete your story questions chart, you can plan the plot or action for your story. You build the plot by adding characters who each try to help the main character.

This is what Hunter did to plan the plot for his add-on story.

Think First, Hunter thought about characters who could help Rabbit.

Choose From his thinking, he chose three characters to help rabbit.

Make Next, Hunter made a story grid. He listed his characters and what they did.

I began with Rabbit. Then I added Ostrich, Little Kangaroo, and Python to my story.

Hunter's Story Grid

Character	Action
Ostrich	used her long neck to try to reach Rabbit
Little Kangaroo	jumped into the hole to try to save Rabbit
Python	tied himself to a tree and lowered himself into the hole

Prewrite ▶ **Gather details.**

1. Think about other characters and their actions.
2. Complete a story grid.

 TEKS 2.17B, 2.18A

Drafting ▶ Beginning Your Story

In the beginning paragraph, you should set up your story. Name the main character, the problem, and the setting.

Here's what Hunter did to write the beginning for his story.

> **Beginning**
> **Middle**
> **Ending**

Review First, Hunter reviewed his story questions chart. This chart names the main character, the problem, and the setting.

Name Hunter then wrote his first sentence. He decided to name the setting and main character in this sentence.

> One morning, Rabbit woke up and began digging.

Add Then he added more sentences that explained the problem.

Remember that the beginning paragraph sets up your story. It should sound interesting or exciting so that readers want to read on.

Hunter's Beginning

> One morning, Rabbit woke up and began digging. He loved to dig, so he dug and dug a deep hole. When he was done, Rabbit had a problem. He couldn't get out!

Draft ▶ **Begin your story.**

1. Review your story questions chart.
2. Write your first sentence naming the main character and setting.
3. Add more sentences that explain the main character's problem.

 TEKS 2.17B, 2.18A, 2.21A(i)
ELPS 5D, 5G

Drafting ▶ Developing the Middle

In the middle part, you develop the plot or action of your add-on story. To do this, show how each new character tries to help the main character.

This is what Hunter did to develop the middle part of his story.

Beginning
Middle
Ending

Review First, Hunter reviewed his story grid.

Show Then he showed how each new character tried to help Rabbit.

I used dialogue and specific action verbs like *stretched* and *hissed* to make this part fun to read.

Draft ▶ **Develop the middle.**

1. Review your story grid.
2. Show how each new character tries to help.
3. Use dialogue and specific action verbs.

Hunter wrote about each new character in a different paragraph. This makes his story easy to follow.

Hunter's Middle Part

"Help me!" Rabbit cried.

Ostrich heard him and looked into the hole. She stretched her long neck and tried to reach Rabbit. Her neck was not long enough.

Little Kangaroo came along. She hopped into the hole. "Jump into my pocket, and we will hop out," she said. Rabbit was too heavy. Little Kangaroo jumped out alone.

"Sssssss," someone hissed. It was Python. He said, "I know what to do." He tied himself to a tree to make a long rope. Then Rabbit climbed up Python and out of the hole.

Drafting ▶ Ending Your Story

In the ending part, you should tell how your main character feels when the problem is finally solved.

Here's how Hunter completed his add-on story.

Beginning

Middle

▶ Ending

Think First, Hunter thought about how his main character would feel.

Write Then he wrote his ending.
  1. The first sentence tells how Rabbit felt.
  2. The second sentence tells how the problem changed him.

I decided that my main character would feel excited.

Hunter's ending paragraph comes after the problem is solved. It tells what the main character learned.

Hunter's Ending

> Rabbit was excited to be out of the hole. He said, "I'll never dig that deep again."

You could turn your add-on story into a book with pictures.

Draft ▶ End your story.

1. Think about how the main character would feel after the problem is solved.
2. Write at least two sentences. In the first one, tell how your main character feels. In the next sentence, tell how he or she has changed.

 TEKS 2.17C
ELPS 1B, 5G

Revising ▶ Improving Your Writing

When you revise, you make sure that your add-on story is clear and complete.

Here's how Hunter revised his story.

Check Hunter checked his first draft using the checklist below as a guide.

Did you review?

✔ 1. Does the beginning name the main character with a problem?

✔ 2. Does the middle add on characters and their actions?

✔ 3. Does the last action solve the problem?

✔ 4. Does the ending tell how the main character felt?

Make He then made any needed changes.

Revise ▶ Improve your writing.

1. Check your story using the checklist above.
2. Make changes by adding or taking out details.

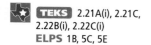
Editing ▶ Checking for Conventions

When you edit your story, you check it for grammar, capitalization, punctuation, and spelling. (See page 452.)

Here's how Hunter edited his story.

Check Hunter edited his story using the checklist below as a guide.

Did you check?

✔ 1. Did you use verbs correctly?

✔ 2. Did you capitalize names and the first word in each sentence?

✔ 3. Did you use correct punctuation (. ? !) after each sentence?

✔ 4. Did you check for spelling?

Correct Then he corrected any errors.

Edit ▶ Check for conventions.

1. Check your story for conventions using the checklist above as a guide.
2. Correct any errors.

Publishing ▶ Sharing Your Story

Write a neat final copy of your story to share.

Rabbit's Big Mistake

One morning, Rabbit woke up and began digging. He loved to dig, so he dug and dug a deep hole. When he was done, Rabbit had a problem. He couldn't get out!

"Help me!" Rabbit cried.

Ostrich heard him and looked into the hole. She stretched her long neck and tried to reach Rabbit. Her neck was not long enough.

Little Kangaroo came along. She hopped into the hole. "Jump into my pocket, and we will hop out," she said. Rabbit was too heavy. Little Kangaroo jumped out alone.

"Sssssss," someone hissed. It was Python. He said, "I know what to do." He tied himself to a tree to make a long rope. Then Rabbit climbed up Python and out of the hole.

Rabbit was excited to be out of the hole. He said, "I'll never dig that deep again."

Publish ▶ Share your story.

Adding Up the Elements of Stories

The words and ideas below describe the main parts of stories.

Action   The action is what happens in a story.

Character   A character is a person or an animal in a story.

Dialogue   Dialogue is what characters say to each other.

Fiction   Fiction is a made-up story.

Moral   A moral is the lesson that a story teaches.

Plot   The plot is what happens.

Problem   The problem is the trouble in a story.

Setting   The setting is the time and place of a story.

Theme   The theme is the main idea or message in a story.

Creating a Play

Plays are fun to write because the writer decides what the characters say and do. Jade turned the nursery rhyme below into a play.

In this chapter, you, too, will learn how to write a play based on a nursery rhyme.

Polly Put the Kettle On

Polly put the kettle on.
Polly put the kettle on.
Polly put the kettle on.
We'll all have tea.
Suki take it off again.
Suki take it off again.
Suki take it off again.
They've all gone away.

Dialogue is what the characters say.
Stage Directions tell what the characters do and how they feel.

Jade's Play

Where Did Everybody Go?

Characters: **Polly and Suki**

Setting: **It is afternoon. Polly and Suki are in the house.**

Dialogue

Suki: Look! Visitors are coming. Polly, put the kettle on. Polly, put the kettle on. Polly, put the kettle on. We'll all have tea.

Polly: (making tea) How many are there? How much tea should I make? (Polly runs to the window to see.)

(Stage Directions)

Polly: Suki, take it off again. Suki, take it off again. Suki, take it off again. They've all gone away!

Suki: (looking out window) What? Where did everybody go?

Prewriting ► Selecting a Topic

To get started, select a nursery rhyme that you would like to turn into a play.

This is what Marta did to select a topic.

List of Topics

Hey Diddle Diddle

Simple Simon

Five Little Ducks

Rose and the Lily

Think   Marta thought about the nursery rhymes that her class read.

List   She listed her favorite ones.

> Choose a nursery rhyme that has at least two characters in it.

Circle   Then Marta circled the rhyme she wanted to turn into a play.

Prewrite ► Select a topic.

1. List your favorite nursery rhymes.
2. Circle the one you will turn into a play.

Prewriting ▶ Gathering Details

To plan your play, think about the characters you will include. Also think about the setting of your play.

Here's what Marta did to gather her first details for her play.

Make　First, Marta made a T-chart. She labeled one side *characters* and the other side *setting*.

Name　Next, she listed the characters and setting for her play.

Details T-Chart

Characters	Setting
Simple Simon pieman	Time: Summer
	Place: On the way to the fair

Prewrite ▶ **Gather details.**

1. Make a T-chart.
2. Name the characters and setting for your play.

Prewriting ▶ Putting Events in Order

The next step is to think of the important events that happen in the nursery rhyme. Knowing these events will help you write your play.

Storyboard

Here's what Marta did to plan the action for her play.

Read Marta read the nursery rhyme so that she knew what happened.

Draw Then Marta drew pictures of the important events in the nursery rhyme. She put the events in time order in a storyboard.

first

Making a storyboard helped me plan the different actions and dialogue in my play.

Your storyboard should have at least four boxes. Otherwise, you may not have enough details to write a play.

Marta ordered her storyboard with the time-order words **first, next, then,** and **last**.

next

then

last

Can I have a taste?

Do you have a penny?

Does anyone have a penny?

Prewrite ▶ **Plan a storyboard.**

1. Read the nursery rhyme.
2. Draw a storyboard of the events in the nursery rhyme. Label it using time-order words.

 **TEKS** 2.17B

Drafting ▶ Beginning Your Play

In the beginning part, name the characters and the setting of your play. Also tell what is happening as the play starts.

This is what Marta did to write the beginning part of her play.

▶ Beginning

Middle

Ending

Review First, Marta reviewed her T-chart from page 245.

Characters	Setting
Simple Simon pieman	Time: Summer Place: On the way to the fair

Write Next, she wrote sentences that tell who the characters are and what is happening.

Plays are fun to write and even more fun to perform. (See page 257.)

The beginning part of Marta's play helps the reader picture who is in the play, where they are, and what they are doing.

Marta's Beginning

Characters: Simple Simon and
a pieman
Setting: It is summer. The place
is on the way to the fair.
Along the way, Simple
Simon meets a pieman.

Draft ▶ **Begin your play.**

1. Review your T-chart from page 245.
2. Write a sentence that tells who the characters are and what is happening to start your play.

Drafting ▶ Developing the Middle

In the middle part, you tell your story by having the characters talk to each other. You also include stage directions when they are needed.

This is what Marta did to develop the middle part of her play.

> Beginning
> **Middle**
> Ending

Review Marta reviewed her storyboard. (See pages 246–247.)

Write Then she wrote the middle part of her play.

> The characters tell the story, so their words are the most important part of my play.

In Marta's play, the stage directions, in parentheses, tell what the characters do or how they feel.

Marta's Main Part

Simple Simon: (shakes hands with the pieman) Your pies look yummy.

Pieman: Would you like to buy one?

Simple Simon: No. I would like to taste one piece.

Pieman: It will cost a penny for a taste.

Simple Simon: (looks through pockets and shoes) I don't have a penny.

Pieman: Then no pie for you.

Simple Simon: Not even a taste?

Pieman: No penny. No taste. No pie!

Draft ▶ **Develop the middle.**

1. Review your storyboard.
2. Write the middle part of your play.

TEKS 2.17B

Drafting ▶ Ending Your Play

In the ending of your play, have the main character say one last important thing.

This is what Marta did to write the ending for her play.

| Beginning |
| Middle |
| ▶ Ending |

Read Marta read the middle part of her play to help her decide what the main character should say and do in the ending.

Write Then she wrote the main character's last line. She added stage directions as needed.

Add Next, Marta added a title. She tried two ways to write it.

1. **Name the characters.**

   Simon and the Pieman

2. **Use a topic detail.**

   Just One Tiny Taste

> Marta's ending fits in with the nursery rhyme and the rest of her play.

Marta's Ending

> **Simple Simon:** (walking off stage, calls to other people going to the fair) Does anyone have a penny so I can try some pie?

> In my ending, I first gave stage directions. Then I had Simple Simon ask a final question.

Draft ▶ **End your play.**

1. Read the middle part of your play.
2. Write the main character's last line. Also add stage directions if needed.

Revising ▶ Improving Your Play

Revise your play to be sure it is clear and easy to follow.

Here's what Marta did to revise her play.

Review Marta reviewed her first draft using the questions below as a guide.

1. Does your beginning tell what is happening as the play starts?

2. In the middle, did you write each character's name before her or his words?

3. Did you have the main character say something important in the ending?

Make She then made the needed changes so her play was clear.

Revise ▶ Improve your play.

1. Check your play using the questions above as a guide.

2. Make changes by adding or taking out details.

Editing ▶ **Checking for Conventions**

Edit your play to be sure it is free of errors.

This is what Marta did to edit her play.

Check Marta checked her play for conventions using the checklist below as a guide.

Correct She then corrected any convention errors.

Did you check?

✔ 1. Did you capitalize proper nouns and the first words of sentences?

✔ 2. Did you end sentences with correct punctuation?

✔ 3. Did you use parentheses ( ) around stage directions?

✔ 4. Did you check your spelling?

Edit ▶ **Check for conventions.**

1. Check your play for conventions using the checklist above as a guide.
2. Correct any errors.

TEKS 2.17E
ELPS 2I, 3E

Publishing ▶ Sharing Your Play

Just One Tiny Taste

Characters: Simple Simon and a pieman

Setting: It is summer. The place is on the way to the fair. Along the way to the fair, Simple Simon meets a pieman.

Simple Simon: (shakes hands with the pieman) Your pies look yummy.

pieman: Would you like to buy one?

Simple Simon: No. I would like to taste one piece.

pieman: It will cost a penny for a taste.

Simple Simon: (looks through pockets and shoes) I don't have a penny.

pieman: Then no pie for you.

Simple Simon: Not even a taste?

pieman: No penny. No taste. No pie!

Simple Simon: (walking off stage, calls to other people going to the fair) Does anyone have a penny so I can try some pie?

Publish ▶ Share your play.

Performing a Play

You can share your play by reading it to your classmates. You can also perform your play as a group. Follow the steps below to perform your play.

Select Select a classmate for each character and for a narrator. (See below.)

Give Give each team member a copy of the play, and decide who gets each part.

Practice Practice reading the play and following the stage directions.

Perform Perform the play by reading it to your audience. (Speak the play if you memorized it.) Follow the stage directions as you go.

The narrator shares the opening part to set the scene for the play.

Narrator: "Just One Tiny Taste" takes place in the summer. Along the way to the fair, Simple Simon meets a pieman.

Writing Poems

Poems come in all shapes and sizes. Some poems rhyme. Some poems follow a certain shape. Other poems even follow the alphabet!

Alec has fun writing poems. He especially likes writing rhyming poems and name poems. You can write these poems, too. This chapter will show you how.

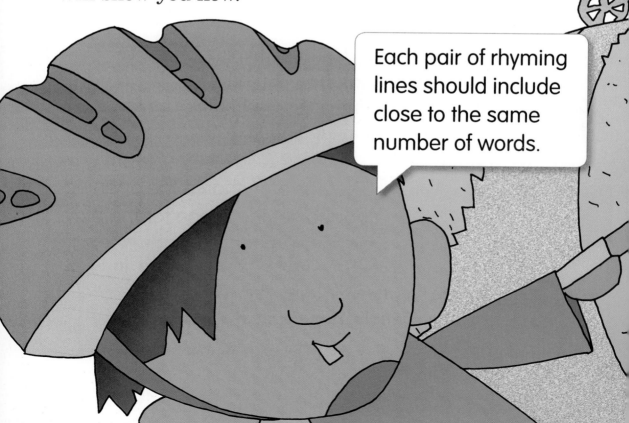

Each pair of rhyming lines should include close to the same number of words.

Alec's Rhyming Poem

Riding

My bike is more fun than TV or a slide.

The tires spin fast wherever I ride.

Kids jump aside when I rush by.

Riding my bike makes me one happy guy.

After You Read

1. **Focus** What is the main idea of this poem?
2. **Organization** Which lines of the poem rhyme?
3. **Ideas** Which detail do you like best?

 **TEKS** 2.17A

Prewriting ▶ Choosing a Topic

Writing a rhyming poem can be fun. To get started, think of an activity that you would like to write about.

Pictures of Activities

Here's what Shayna did to select a topic for her poem.

Draw   Shayna drew pictures of her favorite activities.

State   Then she stated the topic for her poem in a sentence.

I will write my poem about dancing.

Prewrite ▶ Choose a topic.

1. Draw pictures of activities you enjoy.
2. State the topic for your poem in a sentence.

Prewriting ▶ Gathering Details

Gather many details about your activity. This will help you decide what to say in your poem.

> This is what Shayna did to gather details.
>
> **Think** Shayna thought about her five senses: sight, hearing, smell, taste, and touch.
>
> **Write** Then she wrote sentences that described some sensory details about dancing.

Sensory Sentences

> **Dancing**
>
> I **see** the world spin when I twirl.
>
> I **hear** music with a steady beat.
>
> I **smell** fresh air when I dance outside.
>
> I **feel** the wind when I dance.

Prewrite ▶ **Gather details.**

1. Think about your activity.
2. Write sentences about the activity that describe what you see, hear, smell, taste, or feel.

Prewriting ▶ Listing Rhyming Words

Before you write your first draft, you should think of rhyming words that you can use in your poem.

This is what Shayna did to gather rhyming words for her poem.

Choose   Shayna chose special words from her sensory sentences. She wrote them across the top of her paper.

List   Then she listed words that rhyme with each special word.

List of Rhyming Words

dance	twirl	beat	spin
prance	girl	neat	win
chance	whirl	treat	chin
France	swirl	feet	grin

Prewrite ▶ **List rhyming words.**

1. Choose special words from your sensory sentences. Write them at the top of your paper.
2. List words that rhyme with each special word.

Drafting ▶ Writing Your First Draft

Write a poem that tells sensory details about the activity. Make each pair of lines rhyme.

Here's how Shayna wrote her rhyming poem.

Choose   Shayna chose to write a rhyming poem in four lines.

Use   For each pair of lines, she used a special word from her chart at the end of the first line and a rhyming word at the end of the second line.

Sample Rhyming Lines

I love to dance to a drumming beat.
I clap my hands and stomp my feet.

Draft ▶ **Write your first draft.**

1. Decide how many lines to write. Use rhyming words at the end of each pair of lines.
2. Describe what you see, hear, smell, taste, or feel.

 **TEKS** 2.17C, 2.18B
ELPS 1B, 5G

Revising ▶ Improving Your Poem

Make sure that your poem is fun to read. Each pair of lines should sound good together.

This is what Shayna did to revise her rhyming poem.

Use   Shayna used the following checklist to help her review her poem.

Did you review?

✔ 1. Did you write about one activity?

✔ 2. Did you make each pair of lines rhyme?

✔ 3. Did you include sensory details (what you see, hear, smell, taste, or feel)?

Make   Then she made any needed changes.

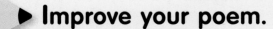

Revise ▶ **Improve your poem.**

1. Use the checklist above to review your poem.
2. Make changes by adding or taking out details.

Editing ▶ Checking for Conventions

Correct writing is easier and more fun to read. Checking for conventions is important. (See page 452.)

This is how Shayna edited her poem.

Check Shayna checked her poem for conventions. She used the checklist below as a guide.

Did you check?

✓ 1. Did you capitalize the pronoun I?

✓ 2. Did you capitalize proper nouns and the first words of sentences?

✓ 3. Did you use complete sentences with correct end punctuation?

✓ 4. Did you check for spelling?

Correct She then corrected any convention errors.

Edit ▶ **Check for conventions.**

1. Check your poem using the checklist above.
2. Correct any errors.

TEKS 2.17E
ELPS 2I, 3E

Publishing ▶ Sharing Your Poem

Shayna's Poem

Shayna Dancing

I love to dance to a Latin beat.

I clap my hands and stomp my feet.

I feel the wind as I spin and twirl.

Look! I'm a happy dancing girl!

Publish ▶ Make a neat final copy.

1. Add a title and make a neat copy of your poem.
2. Read your poem to family and friends.

Creating a Name Poem

A name poem uses the letters in a name to make a list poem.

This is how you start your name poem.

Write   Write your name across the top of a piece of paper.

List   List three or more describing words or sensory detail words for each letter.

Describing Words

S	E	A	N
smart	excited	amusing	nice
scientist	empties the trash	actor	nickname is Champ
speaks Spanish	explores the beach	age 8	never naughty
sweet		an amigo	

TEKS 2.18B
ELPS 2I, 3E

Completing Your Name Poem

To write your name poem, use describing words or sensory detail words from your list. Try to use close to the same number of words in each line.

This is how you write, revise, and publish your poem.

Choose Choose describing words from your chart. Use one or more words in each line.

Check Check your poem for capitalization and spelling.

Make Make a neat final copy to share.

Sean's Name Poem

Speaks Spanish
Explores the beach
Amigo to everyone
Nickname is Champ

Other Kinds of Poems

Try writing these other kinds of poems, too.

ABC Poem

An **ABC poem** uses part of the alphabet to make a list poem.

Amazing

Bubbles

Can

Dance

Everywhere.

Tongue Twister

A **tongue twister** is a short, silly story poem. Most of the words begin with the same sound. This is called **alliteration**.

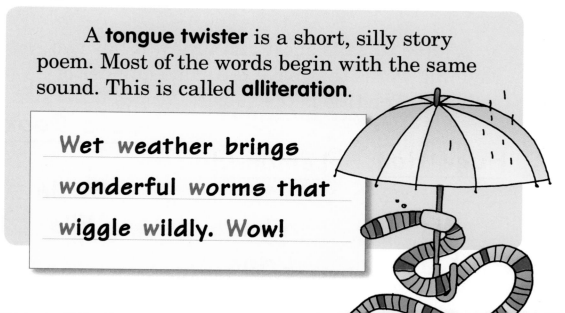

Wet weather brings

wonderful worms that

wiggle wildly. Wow!

Shape Poem

A **shape poem** uses the words of the poem to make the shape of the poem's main idea.

There's a fish! Jumping, splashing, swimming, swish, swish, swish. Look down in the river!

Terse Verse

Terse verse is short and funny. It has two rhyming words that have the same number of syllables. The title is the subject.

Huge Hog

Big
Pig

Lemonade

Pink
Drink

Joke Book

Smile
File

Diamond Poem

This **diamond poem** follows a syllable pattern. (Lines two and six name the subject.)

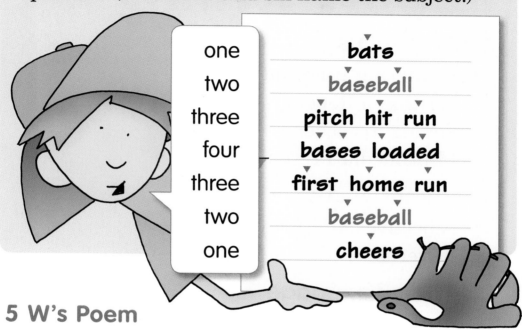

one	**bats**
two	baseball
three	**pitch hit run**
four	**bases loaded**
three	**first home run**
two	baseball
one	**cheers**

5 W's Poem

A **5 W's poem** is five lines long. Each line answers one of the 5 W's (*Who? What? When? Where?* and *Why?*).

My dog	Who?
curls up	What?
on my bed	Where?
every night	When?
because I let him.	Why?

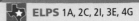

Report Writing

Writing Focus

- Gathering Information
- Writing a Report
- Giving Speeches
- Multimedia Presentation

Grammar Focus

- Adjectives and Articles
- Adverbs

Learning Language

Work with a partner. Read the meanings and share answers to the questions.

1. A **reference** is a book or other source that is used to find information.
   Why is a dictionary a good reference?
2. **Visuals** are things you show, such as pictures or charts, to give information.
   What visuals are in your classroom?
3. To write something out **word for word** means to write exactly what you will say.
   What could you write word for word?

What do you do when you have a question? Of course, you can ask your teachers and parents. You can also go to the library to find an answer. In this section, you will learn how to find information, write a report, create a speech, and create a multimedia presentation.

⭐ **TEKS** 2.24A, 2.24B, 2.25A, 2.25B, 2.25C
ELPS 4G

The Research Process

Creating a Research Plan

owl   bobwhite
eagle   hummingbird
flamingo   jay   duck
parrot   kiwi   heron
penguin   tern   pigeon

I am really interested in hummingbirds.

- **Generate** a list of topics.
- **Choose** a topic.
- **Formulate** questions about your topic.
- **Choose** your sources.

Gathering Information

Books Hummingbirds by Diane Swanson
       Birds by Claude Delafosse
Magazine Birdwatcher's Digest
Internet www.hummingbirds.net

1. What does it look like?
- long, pointy beak
- shiny green, purple, red, orange, brown, and gray feathers
- wings go fast
- 3 1/2 inches long

2. How do they build their nests?
- built by mother bird
- filled with cattail fuzz and dandelion fluff
- sticks and spiderwebs

3. What does it eat?
- nectar from red and orange flowers
- tree sap and insects
- eat while flying

4. What are their eggs like?
- white
- lays two eggs
- size of a pea

- **Gather** evidence from sources and interviews.
- **Use** references to find information.
- **Record** information and answers to your questions in notes, charts, picture graphs, or diagrams.

Synthesizing Information

7. What are some amazing facts?
- the nest can stretch
- fly forward, backward, up, and down
- wings hum when they fly

8. Why do I like this bird?
- beautiful, tiny birds
- fun to watch

- **Review** the answers to your questions.
- **Revise** your topic based on your answers.

Organizing and Presenting Ideas

A hummingbird is ~~a~~ _an_ amazing bird. When it flies, its wings go so fast that they hum. That is how the bird got its name. A hummingbird can fly up, down, forward, and even backward.

The hummingbird is ~~tiney~~ _tiny_. It is about 3 1/2 inches long. Its feathers are mostly brown and gray, but some are shiny green, purple, red,

Humming Wonders

A hummingbird is an amazing bird. When it flies, its wings move so fast that they hum. That is how the bird got its name. A hummingbird can fly up, down, forward, and even backward.

The hummingbird is tiny. It is about 3 1/2 inches long. Its feathers are mostly brown and gray, but some are a shiny green, purple, red, or orange.

When a hummingbird eats, it flies like a helicopter. It pokes its long beak into flowers and drinks nectar. A hummingbird likes orange and red flowers. It also eats tree sap and insects.

...ther bird builds a ...out of tiny sticks and ...s. She fills the nest with ...luff and cattail fuzz. ...ys two white eggs. The ...e size of peas. ...two weeks, the eggs ...chicks are very tiny. ...o feathers. The mother ...cts, sap, and nectar ...babies. They grow ...r three weeks, they

...ngbird seems very ...piderwebs let the nest ...e babies grow! I like ...bird because it is ...ul, and amazing.

- **Write**, **revise**, and **edit** your report.
- **Think** of sounds, actions, and visuals to support your research.
- **Share** your report by giving a speech or a multimedia presentation.

Gathering Information

Ezra and his class were getting ready to write reports. Each student had to choose a bird to write about. Their teacher took the students to the library to learn how to find information for their reports.

The class learned a lot about using the library. You will, too, on the pages that follow.

The Librarian

The librarian knows all about finding information. Be sure to ask the librarian for help whenever you have a question about the library.

You can ask a librarian . . .

- Where can I find a book about ___*(topic)*___ ?
- Can you suggest other books like this one?
- How do I use the computer catalog?
- Where are the reference books?
- What other sources, besides books, does this library have?

practice

Write two questions you have about your school library. Then interview your school librarian.

ELPS 4C

Sections of a Library

Libraries look different, but they all contain the same types of books and material. Here is an example map of a library. Look for signs that label these sections the next time you visit your library.

Library Map

Fiction: This is where you'll find stories and chapter books.

Fiction

Nonfiction: This section has books about real people, places, and things.

Nonfiction

Reference: This is where the atlases, encyclopedias, and dictionaries are kept.

Reference

Checkout Desk

These sections can help you find sources for your research.

Beginner Books: This is where the picture books are.

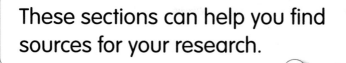

Beginner Books

Computer Catalog

Computer Catalog: This section tells you the titles of every book in the library!

Periodicals

Periodicals: This is where you will find magazines and newspapers.

Media Section

Media Section: This area has CD's, DVD's, and computers.

TEKS 2.25A

The Computer Catalog

A computer catalog gives you three ways to look up a book in a library.

1. If you know the **title** of a book, enter it.
2. If you know the name of the **author**, enter it. A list of the author's books will come up on the computer screen.
3. To find a book on a certain **subject**, enter the subject or a keyword.

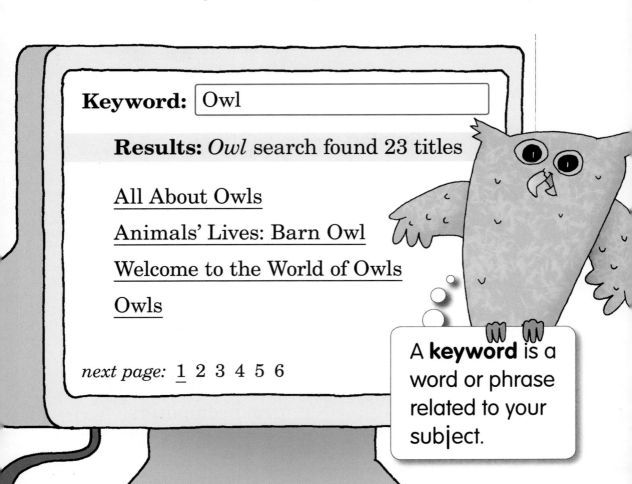

Keyword: Owl

Results: *Owl* search found 23 titles

All About Owls

Animals' Lives: Barn Owl

Welcome to the World of Owls

Owls

next page: <u>1</u> 2 3 4 5 6

A **keyword** is a word or phrase related to your subject.

Call Numbers

To find a nonfiction book, write down the **call number** from the catalog. Use the signs in the library to help you find the book or ask the librarian for help. The picture below shows how to find *All About Owls* on the bookshelf.

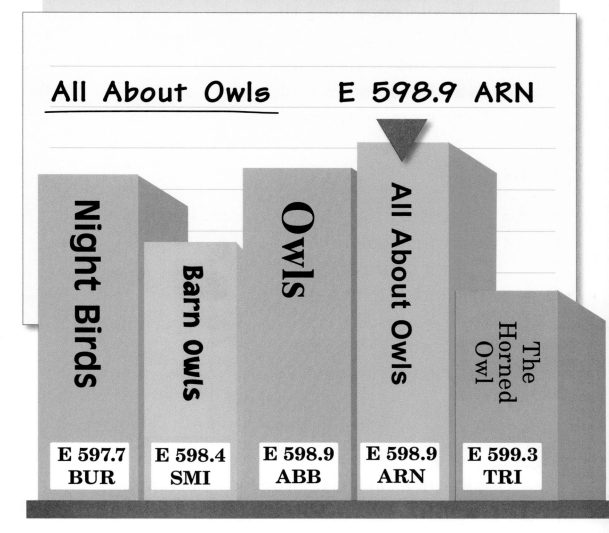

All About Owls   E 598.9 ARN

Night Birds — E 597.7 BUR

Barn Owls — E 598.4 SMI

Owls — E 598.9 ABB

All About Owls — E 598.9 ARN

The Horned Owl — E 599.3 TRI

Parts of a Book

Every book is made up of different parts. Some of these parts give publishing information; other parts help you find chapters or topics in the book.

Front of the Book

- The **title page** lists the book's title and author. It may also list the illustrator.
- The **table of contents** lists the chapters and their page numbers.

Back of the Book

- A **glossary** lists words from the book and their meanings.
- The **index** lists topics from the book in ABC order and gives you their page numbers.

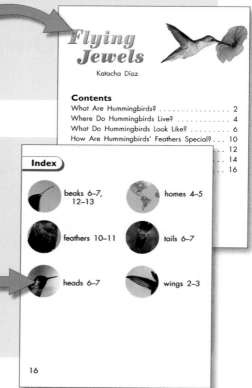

Flying Jewels

Katacha Díaz

Contents

Index

beaks 6–7, 12–13

homes 4–5

feathers 10–11

tails 6–7

heads 6–7

wings 2–3

16

Use the index in this book to locate information about editing and proofreading marks.

Encyclopedia

Encyclopedias are books that contain articles on many topics. The topics are arranged in ABC order. To find information about owls, look in the O book.

Electronic Encyclopedia

Encyclopedias are also found on CD's or on the Internet. Ask your teacher or the librarian to help you use this type of encyclopedia.

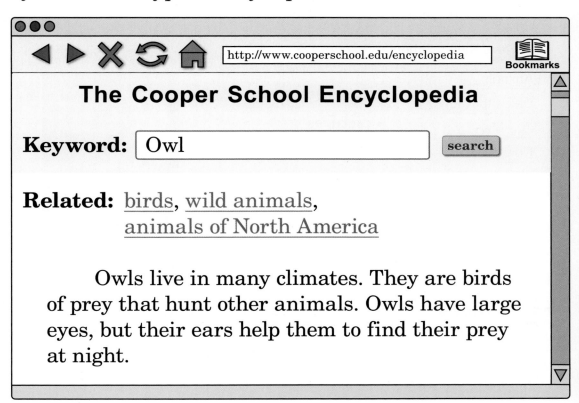

http://www.cooperschool.edu/encyclopedia   **Bookmarks**

The Cooper School Encyclopedia

Keyword: Owl   **search**

Related: birds, wild animals, animals of North America

Owls live in many climates. They are birds of prey that hunt other animals. Owls have large eyes, but their ears help them to find their prey at night.

World Wide Web

Another source of information is the World Wide Web. For example, the Web sites for zoos and rescue centers would probably have interesting details about owls.

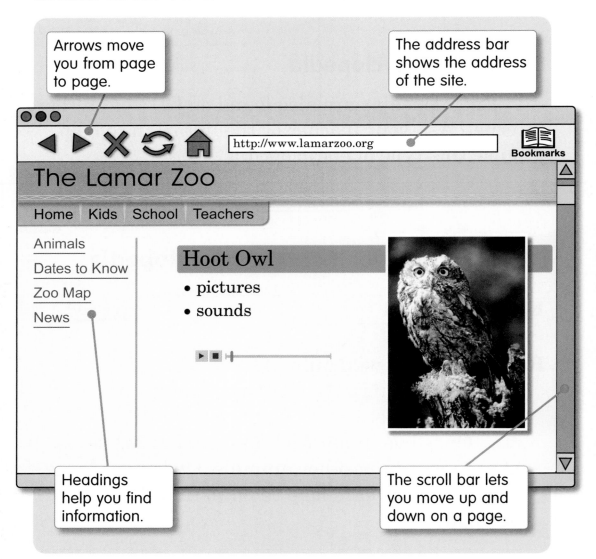

Arrows move you from page to page.

The address bar shows the address of the site.

http://www.lamarzoo.org

Bookmarks

The Lamar Zoo

Home　Kids　School　Teachers

Animals
Dates to Know
Zoo Map
News

Hoot Owl

- pictures
- sounds

Headings help you find information.

The scroll bar lets you move up and down on a page.

Periodicals

Magazines and newspapers are good sources of up-to-date information. New editions come out every month, every week, or every day. See the sample magazine pages below.

Cover

Date — May 2010

Owl World

The Who's Whoooo in the Bird Kingdom

Table of Contents

Table of Contents

The Bird's Word — 5
Better Barns for Owls — 7
From Nest to Egg — 18
Burrowing Owls of the Dakotas — 25

Page number

Article

7

Better Barns for Owls
by Bo Birdwatcher

Some barns make better homes than others. To attract owls to your barn, there are some simple tips you can follow.

Title

Author

 2.19A

Writing a Report

In a report, you can share what you learn about an interesting topic. Tori wrote a report about hummingbirds. It is one of her best pieces of writing. You can write a report, too. This chapter will show you how.

Tori's Report

Humming Wonders

Beginning

    A hummingbird is an amazing bird. When it flies, its wings move so fast that they hum. That is how the bird got its name. A hummingbird can fly up, down, forward, and even backward.

Middle

    The hummingbird is tiny. It is about 3 1/2 inches long. Its feathers are mostly brown and gray, but some are a shiny green, purple, red, or orange.

Tori's Report (continued)

Middle

    When a hummingbird eats, it flies like a helicopter. It pokes its long beak into flowers and drinks nectar. A hummingbird likes orange and red flowers. It also eats tree sap and insects.

Middle

    The mother bird builds a small nest out of tiny sticks and spiderwebs. She fills the nest with dandelion fluff and cattail fuzz. Then she lays two white eggs. The eggs are the size of peas.

Middle

In about two weeks, the eggs hatch. The chicks are very tiny. They have no feathers. The mother gathers insects, sap, and nectar to feed her babies. They grow fast. In two or three weeks, they can fly!

Ending

A hummingbird seems very smart. The spiderwebs let the nest stretch as the babies grow! I like the hummingbird because it is shiny, beautiful, and amazing.

TEKS 2.17A, 2.19A, 2.24A
ELPS 3E

Prewriting ▶ Generating Topics

Brainstorming a list of topics is the first thing you do in report writing. Then you choose a topic to research and think of questions about your topic.

Tori's class brainstormed about different birds. Their teacher wrote the bird's names on the board. Tori decided to write about hummingbirds. She had watched them in her grandmother's yard.

Topic Ideas

owl	bobwhite	
eagle	hummingbird	
flamingo	jay	duck
parrot	kiwi	heron
penguin	tern	pigeon

I am really interested in hummingbirds.

Prewrite ▶ Generate a topic.

1. Brainstorm a list of topics with your class. Then pick one topic to write about.
2. Decide on a topic that truly interests you, and begin thinking of questions about your topic.

Prewriting ▶ Choosing Your Sources

Finding sources to help you answer questions about your topic is the next step.

Tori thought about what she wanted to learn about hummingbirds. She asked her teacher and the librarian for help finding sources of information. Then Tori listed the sources she found in the following way.

Source List

Books	**Hummingbirds** by Diane Swanson
	Birds by Claude Delafosse
Magazine	**Birdwatcher's Digest**
Internet	**www.hummingbirds.net**

 Prewrite ▶ **Choose sources.**

1. Ask your teacher or librarian for help finding sources that will answer your topic questions.
2. Make a list of sources, like the list above.
3. Make sure each source will be helpful by looking at the table of contents, index, or headings.

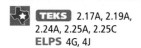 TEKS 2.17A, 2.19A, 2.24A, 2.25A, 2.25C
ELPS 4G, 4J

Prewriting ▶ Formulate Questions

Making a gathering grid can help you to formulate questions and gather evidence or details.

Tori folded a large sheet of paper into eight squares and wrote a question in each. Then she listed facts from her sources under each question.

Gathering Grid

1. What does it look like?	**3. What does it eat?**
• long, pointy beak • shiny green, purple, red, orange, brown, and gray feathers • wings go fast • 3 1/2 inches long	• nectar from red and orange flowers • tree sap and insects • eat while flying
2. How do they build their nests?	**4. What are their eggs like?**
• built by mother bird • filled with cattail fuzz and dandelion fluff • sticks and spiderwebs	• white • lays two eggs • size of a pea

Finally, Tori reviewed the evidence under each question. She revised her topic by deciding which details she wanted to write about.

5. Where does it live?

- North and South America
- in forests and gardens
- near water

7. What are some amazing facts?

- the nest can stretch
- fly forward, backward, up, and down
- wings hum when they fly

6. What are the baby birds like?

- no feathers
- fly in 2–3 weeks

8. Why do I like this bird?

- beautiful, tiny birds
- fun to watch

Prewrite ▶ **Gather evidence.**

1. Make a gathering grid with your questions.
2. Use your sources to find answers.
3. Review your evidence and revise your topic.

TEKS 2.19A, 2.24A, 2.24B, 2.25A, 2.25C
ELPS 2G, 2H, 2I, 3F

Prewriting ▶ Interviewing an Expert

Other people may know about your topic. Tori decided to interview her grandmother, who is an expert on hummingbirds.

Interview Tips

Before the Interview

Think of a person who knows about your topic.

With a parent's help, **set up a time** to interview this person.

Write questions you would like to ask. Leave space after each to write the answers.

During the Interview

Ask questions and listen carefully.

Write the answers on your paper.

After the Interview

Thank the person for talking with you.

Write facts from your notes onto your grid. (See pages 292–293.)

Tori's Interview

1. What do hummingbirds eat?
   —sap and insects
   —drink nectar with a long tongue

2. Where have you seen hummingbirds?
   —at the feeder on the porch
   —near flowers at the nature preserve

3. Why do you like hummingbirds?
   —colored like shiny, bright jewels

4. What is your favorite thing about the hummingbird?
   —fun to watch

Prewrite ▶ **Interview an expert.**

1. Decide on someone to interview about your topic.
2. Plan and carry out the interview. Use all the tips on page 294.

TEKS 2.17B, 2.19A
ELPS 5F

Drafting ▶ Beginning Your Report

The beginning part of a report should get the reader's interest and introduce your topic.

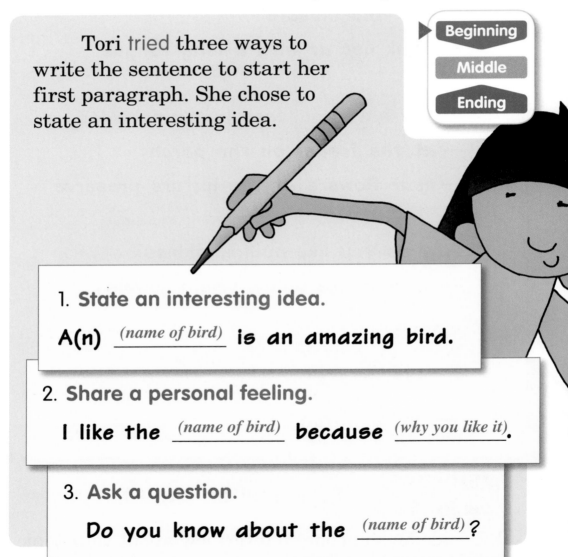

Tori tried three ways to write the sentence to start her first paragraph. She chose to state an interesting idea.

▶ **Beginning**

Middle

Ending

1. **State an interesting idea.**

   A(n) _(name of bird)_ **is an amazing bird.**

2. **Share a personal feeling.**

   I like the _(name of bird)_ **because** _(why you like it)_.

3. **Ask a question.**

   Do you know about the _(name of bird)_**?**

Tori started her first paragraph with an interesting idea. Then she reviewed her grid and chose two facts to support the first sentence. Her goal was to make her topic sound really interesting.

The beginning paragraph introduces the topic and shares interesting facts.

Tori's Beginning Paragraph

A hummingbird is a amazing bird. When it flies, its wings hum. That is how the bird got its name. A hummingbird can fly up down forward and backward.

Draft ▶ Write your beginning.

1. Use your best first sentence to start your beginning paragraph.
2. Review the questions and answers in your gathering grid. Choose two or three interesting facts that support the beginning sentence.

TEKS 2.17B, 2.19A, 2.26
ELPS 5G

Drafting ▶ Creating the Middle Part

Your middle paragraphs should explain and describe your topic.

Tori reviewed her grid and chose which main ideas to include in her report. She put the ideas in order. Then she wrote her middle paragraphs. She wrote about a different main idea in each paragraph. She included details from her grid to support each main idea.

Beginning

▶ Middle

Ending

Tori's Main Ideas

1. Describe the bird's body.
2. Explain what and how it eats.
3. Tell about its nest and eggs.
4. Tell about the babies.

Tori used a lot of details from her gathering grid in this paragraph.

Tori's First Middle Paragraph

> The hummingbird is tiney. It is about 3 1/2 inches long Its feathers are mostly brown and gray, but some are a shiny green, purple, red, or orange.

Draft ▶ Create the middle part.

1. Review your gathering grid. Choose four main ideas to include in your report.
2. Write a paragraph for each main idea. Support each main idea with details from your grid.

 **TEKS** 2.17B, 2.19A, ELPS 4K, 5G

Drafting ▶ Ending Your Report

Your ending paragraph should bring your report to a close.

Tori reviewed her ideas from her grid for any amazing details she hadn't used. She started the final paragraph with one of these ideas. Then she finished her paragraph by telling why she likes hummingbirds.

Beginning

Middle

▶ Ending

Ending Ideas

7. What are some amazing facts?

- the nest can stretch
- fly forward, backward, up, and down
- wings hum when they fly

8. Why do I like this bird?

- beautiful, tiny birds
- fun to watch

Tori's Ending Paragraph

A hummingbird seems very smart. The spiderwebs let the nest stretch as the babies grow! I like the hummingbird because it is shiny, beautiful, and amazing.

Draft ▶ **End your report.**

1. List interesting ideas from your gathering grid that you haven't used yet.
2. Start with an amazing idea from your list.
3. Finish your paragraph by telling why you like your topic.

Revising for Focus

When you revise, you try to make your writing better. You might need to take out some ideas to make your topic more focused.

These are the things Tori did to revise her report for focus.

Read Tori read her first draft. She made sure that each paragraph was focused on one main idea.

Decide Tori decided that some of the information in her report did not belong.

Mark Tori used the take out ( ) editing symbol to remove extra ideas.

My third paragraph had more than one main idea.

TEKS 2.17C, 2.19A, 2.26
ELPS 1B, 4K, 5G

This paragraph is about what hummingbirds eat, so Tori took out the detail about where they live.

Tori's Revising

> When a hummingbird eats, it flies like a helicopter. It pokes its long beak into flowers and drinks nectar. A hummingbird likes orange and red flowers. It also eats tree sap and insects. ~~It lives close to the water in forests and gardens.~~

Revise ▶ Improve your focus.

1. Review your first draft. Make sure each paragraph is focused on one main idea.
2. Revise your topic by taking out ideas that do not belong. Use the take out (⟋) editing symbol.

TEKS 2.17C, 2.19A
ELPS 1B, 4K, 5F, 5G

Texas Traits

Revising for Organization

When you revise for organization, you make sure your ideas are in order and easy to follow.

These are the things that Tori did to revise the organization in her report.

Review   Tori reviewed her report for organization. She asked herself three questions:

1. Do I have a clear beginning, middle, and ending?
2. Does the order of my ideas make sense?
3. Do my ideas flow smoothly from one to the next?

Make   Tori made her changes.

I added words in my fourth and fifth paragraphs to help my ideas flow more smoothly.

Tori's Revising

The mother builds a small nest

out of tiny sticks and spiderwebs.

She fills the nest with dandelion fluff

and cattail fuzz. ∧Then She lays two white

eggs. The eggs are the size of peas.

In about two weeks,
∧The eggs hatch. The chicks are

very tiny. The mother gathers food

for her babies. They grow fast. In two

or three weeks, they can fly!

Revise ▶ Improve your organization.

1. Review your report for organization. Use the
   questions on page 304 to help you.
2. Make any needed changes.

TEKS 2.17C, 2.19A
ELPS 1B, 2I, 3E, 4J, 5G

Revising for Development of Ideas

When you revise for ideas, you make sure your main ideas are supported with interesting details.

These are the things that Tori did to develop the ideas in her report.

Read   Tori read her report to a partner.

Listen   She asked for suggestions and listened to what her partner said.

> I would like to know more details about the baby hummingbirds.

Make   Tori used her partner's suggestions to make changes.

> I added two new details to develop the ideas in my fifth paragraph.

Tori's Revising

In about two weeks,
The eggs hatch. The chicks are
They have no feathers.
very tiny. The mother gathers ~~food~~
insects, sap, and nectar to feed
~~for~~ her babies. They grow fast. In two

or three weeks, they can fly!

Revise ▶ Develop your ideas.

1. Read your report to a partner. Ask your partner how you can improve your ideas.
2. Listen to your partner. Then revise your draft. Make sure your ideas are clear and detailed.

TEKS 2.17C, 2.19A
ELPS 1B, 2I, 3E, 4K

Revising for Voice

When you revise for voice, you make sure that you sound confident and excited about your topic. If you sound interested, then your reader will be interested, too!

Here's what Tori did to revise her writing for voice.

Read Tori reread her first draft. She asked herself two questions:

> 1. Do I sound confident in every part?
> 2. Do I sound excited about my topic?

Ask She also asked a partner to check her report for voice.

Make Tori made any needed changes.

> I added words to my beginning paragraph to show my interest.

Tori's Revising

A hummingbird is a amazing
bird. When it flies, its wings ∧ hum.
move so fast that they

That is how the bird got its name. A

hummingbird can fly up down forward

and ∧ backward.
even

Make sure you sound excited about your topic!

Revise ▶ **Improve your voice.**

1. Reread your report to be sure that you sound confident and excited about your topic.
2. Ask a partner to check your draft for voice.
3. Make any needed changes.

 **TEKS** 2.21A(iii)
ELPS 21, 3E, 4C

Texas Traits ☆ Editing for Conventions

Grammar

When you edit for grammar, you make sure you use words correctly.

Which words describe people or things?

An **adjective** is a word that describes a noun or pronoun. You can use an adjective to tell more about a person, place, or thing. The words *a*, *an*, and *the* are special adjectives. These words are called **articles**.

Adjectives: The **funny** clown wore **big** shoes.

Articles: An owl and **a** robin live in **the** tree.

Grammar Practice

Talk It Over With a partner, think of adjectives for each blank line in the paragraph below. Then find the articles. Write them on a piece of paper.

At lunchtime, I sit at a _____ table. Then I eat my _____ lunch. My lunch usually has a _____ sandwich, some _____ carrots, and a _____ apple. It is important to eat three _____ meals every day.

Which words describe actions?

An **adverb** is a word that describes a verb. You can use an adverb to tell when, where, or how an action happens.

When: Carmelo finished the race **first**.

Where: He enjoyed running **outside**.

How: Carmelo ran **quickly** and **quietly**.

Grammar Practice

Talk It Over With a partner, think of adverbs for each blank line in the paragraph below. Write the adverbs on a piece of paper.

_____*(when)*_____ , we went to the pet store. The puppies jumped _____*(how)*_____ , and the kittens climbed _____*(how)*_____ . The birds flew _____*(where)*_____ to a special perch. I want to go back again _____*(when)*_____ !

Learning Language

Write the following words on index cards: *carefully, green, today, sharp, pretty, slowly, there, old, loudly, small*. Work with a partner to sort the words into an adjectives pile and an adverbs pile. Then practice using the words in sentences.

TEKS 2.19A, 2.21A(iii), 2.21A(iv), 2.22B(i), 2.22C(i)
ELPS 5C, 5E

Texas Traits Editing for Conventions

After revising, check your report for conventions. Correct any grammar, capitalization, punctuation, and spelling errors. (See page 452.)

Tori edited her report for conventions using the checklist below as a guide. Next, she corrected any errors she found.

Did you check?

✔ 1. Did you use adjectives, articles, and adverbs correctly?

✔ 2. Did you indent the beginning of each paragraph?

✔ 3. Did you capitalize the first word in each sentence?

✔ 4. Did you capitalize names?

✔ 5. Did you put an end punctuation mark after each sentence?

✔ 6. Did you use commas between words in a series?

✔ 7. Did you check your spelling?

Use **a** in front of words that start with a consonant.
Use **an** before words that start with a vowel.

Tori's Editing

A hummingbird is ~~a~~ *an* amazing
bird. When it flies, its wings go so
fast that they hum. That is how the
bird got its name. A hummingbird
can fly up, down, forward, and even
backward.

The hummingbird is ~~tiney~~ *tiny*. It is
about 3 1/2 inches long. Its feathers
are mostly brown and gray, but
some are shiny green, purple, red,
or orange.

Edit ▶ **Check for conventions.**

1. Edit your report. Use the checklist on page 312.
2. Correct any errors you find.

TEKS 2.17C, 2.17E, 2.19A
ELPS 2I, 3E

Publishing ▶ Creating a Title

Adding a title helps you introduce the report to your readers.

Tori wrote three different titles. She chose her favorite one and starred it.

1. **Name your topic.**

   Hummingbirds

2. **Describe your topic.**

   Tiny, Shiny Birds

3. **Be creative.**

   Humming Wonders *

Publish ▶ Create a title.

1. Try the three ways above to write a title.
2. Choose your favorite one and share it with your class.

Publishing ▶ **Sharing Your Final Copy**

You can neatly print your report or you can make a final copy on a computer.

Tori used a computer to make a final copy of her report. She shared it with her class.

Tori's Final Report

Humming Wonders

A hummingbird is an amazing bird. When it flies, its wings move so fast that they hum. That is how the bird got its name. A hummingbird can fly up, down, forward, and even backward.

The hummingbird is tiny. It is about 3 1/2 inches long. Its feathers are mostly brown and gray, but some are a shiny green, purple, red, or orange.

When a hummingbird eats, it flies like a helicopter. It pokes its long beak into flowers and drinks nectar. A hummingbird likes orange and red flowers. It also eats tree sap and insects.

...ther bird builds a ...out of tiny sticks and ... She fills the nest with ...uff and cattail fuzz. ...ys two white eggs. The ...e size of peas. ...two weeks, the eggs ...chicks are very tiny. ...o feathers. The mother ...cts, sap, and nectar to ...bies. They grow fast. In ...weeks, they can fly! ...ngbird seems very ...piderwebs let the nest ...e babies grow! I like ...bird because it is ...ul, and amazing.

Publish ▶ **Share your final copy.**

TEKS 2.17E, 2.27
ELPS 3F

Giving Speeches

Paco decided that giving a speech would be a good way to share his report on owls with his class. First, he thought of what he would say. Then he added pictures and actions to make his speech exciting.

This chapter will show you how Paco turned his report into a great speech on owls. You can turn your report into a great speech, too!

Paco's Report

Owls

It's no wonder I have never seen an owl! Most owls are nocturnal. That means they hunt at night. Owls have special body parts that help them survive in the dark.

Owls see very well. But their eyes are not much use without their necks. This is because owls can't move their eyes around. An owl must move its entire head in the direction it wants to see.

Owls also have great hearing. Some people think that the tufts of feathers on an owl's head are ears. The ears are actually hidden under its feathers.

Maybe one night I will finally see an owl. But with its great senses, it will probably see and hear me first!

 TEKS 2.25A, 2.27
ELPS 3F, 4J, 4K

Prewriting ▶ Planning Your Speech

Plan your speech by gathering information and organizing it into the main parts of your speech.

First, Paco reread his report on owls and gathered important details to include in his speech.

Next, Paco thought about the main parts of a speech. He organized his details into the beginning, middle, and ending.

Beginning	Name your topic and get the listeners' attention.
Middle	Share the main facts about the topic. Support the facts with pictures and actions.
Ending	Tell why the topic is important.

Prewrite ▶ **Gather and organize details.**

1. Gather information from your report or from another source.
2. Plan the main parts of your speech. Think of pictures and actions that support your ideas.

Drafting ▶ Preparing Your Speech

You can write your speech out word for word, or you may prepare it on note cards.

Paco made note cards. On each card, he wrote what he would say and what he would do.

Beginning

What is your topic?

1.	Say	Do
	• Owls are amazing night birds • They have special body parts	• Smile • Relax

Middle

What are the main facts?

2.	Say	Do
	• Eyes see very well but do not move • Very good hearing • Ear tufts: not ears	• Act out head turn • Show pictures

Ending

Why is your topic important?

3.	Say	Do
	• Great senses • Hope I see one • Thank you	• Look at audience

Draft ▶ Prepare your speech.

1. Look over your details and your plan.
2. Make note cards that tell what you will say and do. (Or write out your speech word for word.)

TEKS 2.17C, 2.27
ELPS 3F, 4K, 5C

Revising and Editing

When you finish writing your speech or note cards, you are ready to revise and edit it. Your goal is to make your speech clear and interesting.

Paco reviewed his note cards and practiced giving his speech out loud. He found ways to improve his speech. Then he checked his note cards for conventions. (See page 452.)

(See page 452.)

Revise ▶ Improve your speech.

1. Did you include the important ideas?
2. Are your ideas clear and in the right order?
3. Did you include pictures and actions to support your ideas?

Edit ▶ Check for conventions.

4. Make sure your speech is neat and easy to read.
5. Check your speech for grammar, capitalization, punctuation, and spelling.

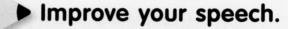

Publishing ▶ Giving Your Speech

Before you give your speech, you should practice it many times. (See the tips below.) It is easier to give a good speech once you know it well.

Paco practiced his speech for his family. When he gave his speech in school, he was careful to speak slowly, clearly, and loudly. He also tried to relax and enjoy himself.

Practice Tips

Use your note cards or paper as you practice your speech.

Support your ideas by showing pictures and acting things out.

Say your speech again and again until you know it by heart.

Publish ▶ Give your speech.

1. Look at your audience.
2. Speak slowly, clearly, and loudly.
3. Relax, smile, and enjoy giving your speech.

TEKS 2.27
ELPS 3F

Multimedia Presentation

Have you ever seen a slide show on a computer? Tori decided to turn her report on hummingbirds into a slide show. She added actions to make her slide show extra fun.

You can make a slide show with your report, too. This chapter will show you how.

Prewriting ▶ Planning Your Slide Show

Plan your slide show carefully and gather a lot of ideas. You can use your report or another source.

Tori made a slide grid. She wrote the main ideas for each slide. Then she added ideas for pictures, sounds, and actions.

Part of Slide Grid

main ideas	pictures	sounds	actions
1. amazing bird (title, paragraph 1)	hummingbird by flower	humming	flying in different directions
2. tiny and shiny (paragraph 2)	big picture of a hummingbird	louder humming	show the bird's size
3. eat nectar (paragraph 3)	bird with beak in flower	humming	hovering, eating

Prewrite ▶ Plan your slide show.

1. Make your own slide grid using information from your report or another source.
2. Write the main idea for each slide.
3. Add ideas for pictures, sounds, and actions.

TEKS 2.25C, 2.27
ELPS 3F, 5G

Prewriting ▶ Creating a Storyboard

Next, make a storyboard. Show the words and pictures that will go on each slide.

Tori made this storyboard. She used her grid and her report for ideas.

Part of Storyboard

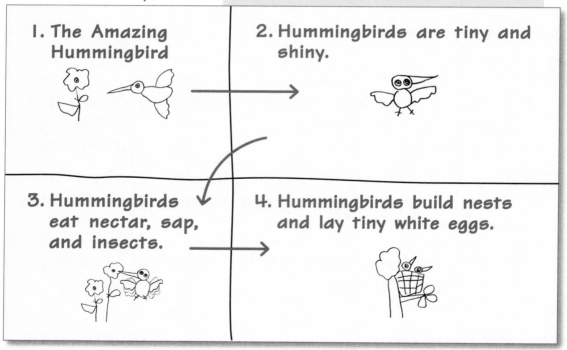

1. The Amazing Hummingbird

2. Hummingbirds are tiny and shiny.

3. Hummingbirds eat nectar, sap, and insects.

4. Hummingbirds build nests and lay tiny white eggs.

Prewrite ▶ Create your storyboard.

1. Create each slide using your grid as a guide.
2. Write the main ideas and pictures that you will include on each slide.

Prewriting ▶ Adding Drama

Finally, add notes about sounds and actions you will perform to dramatize your presentation.

> Tori added sounds and actions to support her ideas. She wrote notes on her storyboard.

Part of Storyboard

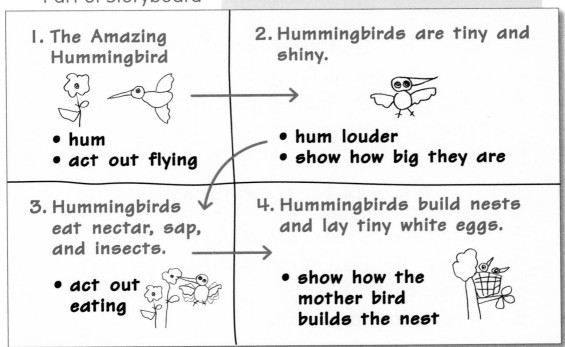

1. The Amazing Hummingbird
   • hum
   • act out flying

2. Hummingbirds are tiny and shiny.
   • hum louder
   • show how big they are

3. Hummingbirds eat nectar, sap, and insects.
   • act out eating

4. Hummingbirds build nests and lay tiny white eggs.
   • show how the mother bird builds the nest

Prewrite ▶ **Dramatize your presentation.**

1. Add notes to each part of your storyboard.
2. Write the sounds you will make and the actions you will perform during your presentation.

 **TEKS** 2.17E, 2.27
ELPS 2I, 3E, 3F, 4K, 5C

Draft ▶ Create your slides and notes.

1. Use a computer program to make your slides. Include words and pictures.
2. Make an index card for each slide. Write what you will say and do while showing each slide.

Revise ▶ Improve your presentation.

3. Did you include all the important ideas?
4. Did you put the slides in the right order?
5. Do the pictures, sounds, and actions support your ideas?

Edit ▶ Check for conventions.

6. Did you spell words correctly?
7. Did you capitalize names and the first words of sentences?
8. Did you use end punctuation?

Publish ▶ Share your slide show.

9. Practice giving your presentation using your computer slides and index cards.
10. Give your presentation in class or at home.

The Tools of Language

Learning Language

Work with a partner. Read the meanings and share your answers.

1. **Language** is what you use to communicate, or speak, to others.
   What languages do you speak?

2. **Directions** tell you the steps for doing something or going somewhere.
   Follow your partner's directions for how to tie a shoe.

3. When you **sound out** a word, you say each sound to figure out how to say the word.
   Sound out the word *flower*.

ELPS 1C, 2B, 2C, 4A

Learning Language
Language Strategies

You hear new words every day. Here are some ideas to help you understand, remember, and use the new words that you hear.

Listen for Language Patterns

Notice how the same letters make the same sounds. Use what you know about sounds to say new words correctly.

You hear: The **sh**eep sit on the **gr**ass.
You can say: I will **sh**are my **gr**apes.

Try It Turn to a partner. Say two more sentences with **sh** and **gr** words.

Use Academic Language

Your teacher may use a word that you do not know. Stretch out the sounds in the word. Then say it aloud to help you remember it.

You hear: The earth orbits the sun.
You repeat: o-r-b-i-t-s, orbits

Try It Listen for words in class that you do not understand. Sound out the words and repeat them to yourself.

Teach a Friend

To remember new words, use them to teach someone you know. You can teach your friends, classmates, and family members.

You hear: The president of a country is the leader.
You can say: The first president of the United States was George Washington.

Try It Use a new word to share something you learned with a friend.

Take Notes or Draw a Picture

To understand and remember a new word, write down the word and its meaning. Then draw a picture of it.

You hear: Plants get water through their roots.
You can write: roots—plant parts that grow in soil
You can draw: a picture of a plant with roots

Try It Write a new word in your notebook. Write notes about its meaning. Then draw a picture of it.

Language of the Writing Process

Read each of the words. Then read about what they mean.

Prewrite ▶ When you prewrite, you plan your writing. You decide what you will write about, who you will write for, and why you will write.

Draft ▶ When you draft, you begin writing about your topic. You organize and support your ideas with details.

Revise ▶ Revising means changing your writing to make it better. You make sure that you wrote about your topic in a clear, organized, and interesting way.

Edit ▶ When you edit, you find and fix mistakes in grammar, capitalization, punctuation, and spelling.

Publish ▶ Finally it is time to publish, or share, your writing. Make a neat, final copy and present it to your audience.

Vocabulary: Writing Process

process	prewrite	draft
revise	edit	publish

1 **Say the word.** Listen and read along as your teacher reads the words aloud. Then repeat each word. Some words have silent letters such as the *k* in *know*. Which word has a silent letter? Practice pronouncing this word with a partner.

2 **Discover the meaning.** With a partner, make a T-chart. Write the words that you know in one column. Then write each word's meaning.

3 **Learn more.** Listen as your teacher explains the meaning of each word. Retell the word meanings to a partner. Then add the words you did not know to your T-chart.

4 **Show your understanding.** Listen as your teacher reads the question below. Answer the question in your notebook.

• Are you editing or publishing when you share your writing?

5 **Write it, show it.** Add words and drawings to your T-chart to help you remember the words.

The Writing Process in Action

You know lots of words you can use to talk about the writing process. Now let's see the process in action! Follow along as your teacher gives you directions for how to do each step. Then write together, using the questions below.

Prewrite

1. What do you like about your favorite activity?
2. Who will you write for and why?

Draft

1. How will you organize your ideas?
2. What details support your ideas?

The Writing Process in Action

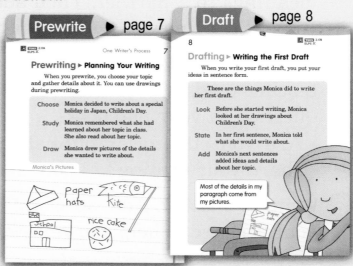

These pages from the first unit in your book show the writing process in action.

Prewrite ▶ page 7

One Writer's Process   7

Prewriting ▶ Planning Your Writing

When you prewrite, you choose your topic and gather details about it. You can use drawings during prewriting.

Choose   Monica decided to write about a special holiday in Japan, Children's Day.

Study   Monica remembered what she had learned about her topic in class. She also read about her topic.

Draw   Monica drew pictures of the details she wanted to write about.

Monica's Pictures

Paper hats   Kite   School   rice cake

Draft ▶ page 8

8

Drafting ▶ Writing the First Draft

When you write your first draft, you put your ideas in sentence form.

These are the things Monica did to write her first draft.

Look   Before she started writing, Monica looked at her drawings about Children's Day.

State   In her first sentence, Monica told what she would write about.

Add   Monica's next sentences added ideas and details about her topic.

Most of the details in my paragraph come from my pictures.

Revise

1. Did you write only about your topic?
2. Are there any sentences you should add or take out?

Edit

1. Did you check that your grammar, spelling, capitalization, and punctuation are correct?
2. Does each sentence make sense?

Publish

1. Is your writing neat and easy to read?

 Turn and Talk

Talk to a classmate about the step you think is most important.

Example: The most important step is _____.

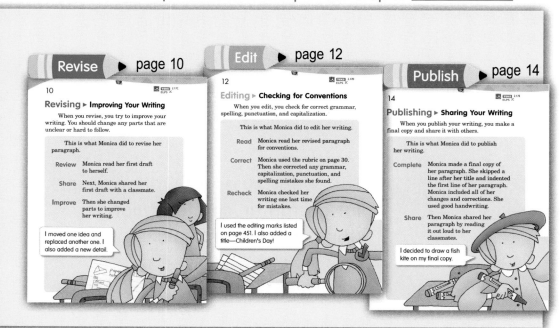

ELPS 4C

Texas Traits

Language of the
Writing Traits

Read each of these words. Then read about what they mean.

Focus — Make sure all of your ideas are about one main idea, or topic.

Organization — Put your writing in order. Make sure the ideas are easy to follow.

Development of Ideas — Use interesting details to develop the ideas in your writing.

Voice — Sound confident and interested in your topic.

Conventions — Follow the rules for writing. Check for grammar, capitalization, punctuation, and spelling.

Vocabulary: Writing Traits

| traits | focus | organization |
| development | voice | conventions |

1. **Say the word.** Listen as your teacher reads the words aloud. Then repeat each word.

2. **Discover the meaning.** Discuss the meanings of words you already know with a partner. Write sentences in your notebook using each of the words.

3. **Learn more.** Listen as your teacher explains the meaning of each word. Retell the word meanings to a partner. Then write a sentence using each new word you learn.

4. **Show your understanding.** Listen as your teacher reads the questions below. Answer them in your notebook.
   - What are examples of rules for writing?
   - Why is developing ideas important?

5. **Write it, show it.** In your notebook, add notes and drawings that will help you remember the vocabulary words.

ELPS 2G, 2I, 3E, 3H

Language of Descriptive Writing

Descriptive writing describes something. It creates a picture of a topic in the reader's mind. A descriptive paragraph has a topic sentence, body sentences, and a closing sentence.

Descriptive Paragraph Organization

Beginning

Middle

Ending

The topic sentence tells what the paragraph is about.

The body sentences describe the topic.

The closing sentence tells how you feel about the topic.

Turn and Talk

Describe your first day of school to a partner.

On my first day of school, I _____.

Vocabulary: Descriptive Writing

topic sentence	**body sentence**	**closing sentence**
detail	**descriptive**	**curriculum**

1 **Say the word.** Listen as your teacher reads the words aloud. Then repeat each word.

2 **Discover the meaning.** With a partner, look at the writing model on page 41. Write down vocabulary words that you see and discuss what you think they mean.

3 **Learn more.** Listen as your teacher explains the meaning of each word. Retell the word meanings to a partner. Then find examples of the words in the writing model on page 41.

4 **Show your understanding.** Listen as your teacher reads the questions below. Answer them in your notebook.
- Would you start your writing with a topic sentence or a closing sentence? Why?
- How can details help a writer describe?

5 **Write it, show it.** Write the vocabulary words and their meanings in your notebook. Include pictures and words to help you remember what they mean.

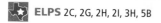 ELPS 2C, 2G, 2H, 2I, 3H, 5B

Reading the Descriptive Model

What Do You Know?

Next you will read "My Teammate Marty," a descriptive paragraph on page 41 about a boy on a soccer team. Are you on a team? What are your teammates like?

Listening

Listen as your teacher or a classmate reads "My Teammate Marty" aloud. As you listen, write down whom or what the paragraph describes. Be prepared to answer the questions below.

1. Who is Marty?
2. What does Marty look like?
3. What does Marty act like? How do you know?

Key Describing Words

blue	brown	white
quickly	fast	great

Look at the words in the box. Listen as your teacher reads them aloud. Practice using one or more of the words to describe something in the classroom to a partner. Then write your sentences in your notebook.

Read Along

Now it's your turn to read. Turn to page 41. As your teacher reads aloud, follow along in your book.

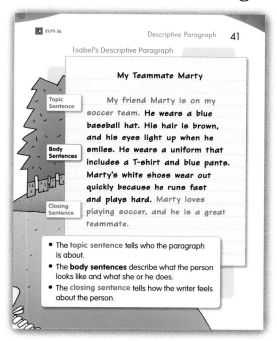

ELPS 5G

Descriptive Paragraph 41

Isabel's Descriptive Paragraph

My Teammate Marty

Topic Sentence

My friend Marty is on my soccer team. He wears a blue baseball hat. His hair is brown, and his eyes light up when he smiles. He wears a uniform that includes a T-shirt and blue pants. Marty's white shoes wear out quickly because he runs fast and plays hard. Marty loves playing soccer, and he is a great teammate.

Body Sentences

Closing Sentence

- The topic sentence tells who the paragraph is about.
- The body sentences describe what the person looks like and what she or he does.
- The closing sentence tells how the writer feels about the person.

After Reading

Sometimes a writer gives information without actually writing it. Explain to a partner how you know that Marty is a good teammate.

ELPS 2G, 2H, 2I, 3E, 3I

Oral Language: Descriptive Writing

The people who listen to you or read your writing are your audience. When you write or speak, use words your audience will understand.

Try It Read the situation below. Then choose two audiences from the bottom of the page. Discuss with a partner how your description might be different for each audience.

Situation

You went on a field trip to the zoo. The zookeeper showed you a hedgehog. You even got to touch it! Describe what the hedgehog was like and how you felt.

Audiences

- The zookeeper
- A three-year-old neighbor
- Your teacher

Effective Talk

Answers to questions can be short or long. Including details in an answer helps your audience better understand you. The question below is answered three ways. The answer with the most details is the most complete.

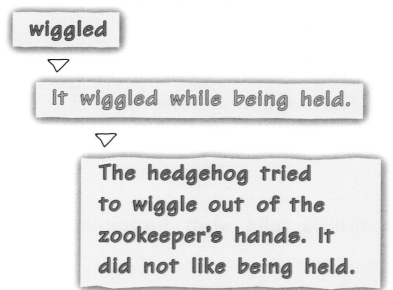

How did the hedgehog act?

wiggled

It wiggled while being held.

The hedgehog tried to wiggle out of the zookeeper's hands. It did not like being held.

Try IT Have you ever seen an interesting animal? Describe it to a partner. Tell where you were, what it was like, and how you felt.

Language of Narrative Writing

Narrative writing is writing that tells a story. All narrative writing has a beginning, middle, and ending. A personal narrative tells a true story about something that happened to you.

Personal Narrative Organization

Beginning

Middle

Ending

The beginning tells what the story will be about.

The middle tells what happened in order.

The ending tells what you learned or how you felt.

Turn and Talk

Share about a time you felt nervous.

I felt very nervous when _____.

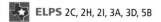
Vocabulary: Narrative Writing

narrative	time line	experience
beginning	middle	ending

1 **Say the word.** Listen as your teacher reads the words aloud. Then repeat each word. Some words have a long vowel sound like the *i* in *prize*. Which words have a long *i* sound? Practice pronouncing these words with a partner.

2 **Discover the meaning.** Discuss the meaning of the words you know with a partner. In your notebook, write the words and their meanings.

3 **Learn more.** Listen as your teacher explains the meaning of each word. Retell the word meanings to a partner. Add the words and meanings you learned to your notebook.

4 **Show your understanding.** Listen as your teacher reads the question below. Answer the question in your notebook.
- What is an example of an experience?

5 **Write it, show it.** Return to your notebook and add words and pictures to help you remember the meanings of the words.

ELPS 2C, 2G, 2H, 2I, 3G, 3H, 4A

Reading the Narrative Model

What Do You Know?

Next you will read "Standing Rock State Park," a personal narrative on page 84 about Kelsey's experience at a state park. Would you like to go to a state park? What would you do there?

Listening

Listen as your teacher or a classmate reads "Standing Rock State Park" aloud. As you listen, write down your thoughts about Kelsey's experience. Then discuss the questions below with a partner.

1. How does Kelsey feel about her experience?
2. What happens first, next, and last in this narrative?

Key Narrative Words

went	through	then
about	found	could

Look at the words in the box. Listen as your teacher reads them aloud. Find the words in the narrative on page 84. Notice that the letters *ou* make different sounds in some words. Sound out the words. Then write them in your notebook.

Read Along

Now it's your turn to read. Turn to page 84. As your teacher reads aloud, follow along in your book.

84   TEKS 2.17E
                                      ELPS 3E

Publishing ▸ **Sharing Your Narrative**

Standing Rock State Park

Last summer, my parents and I went to Standing Rock State Park. We walked on trails through stone cliffs. Waterfalls fell over the high rocks. I saw fuzzy green moss on the edge of the path. Then I yelled, "I hear something really strange!"

Inside a garbage can, I found a raccoon. "There's a baby raccoon here!" I shouted. Dad and Mom just wanted to keep walking. I was mad because no one believed me. Who cared about seeing another waterfall? I wanted to help the raccoon!

At the end of our hike, Dad looked in the garbage can and saw my raccoon! Then Dad found a park ranger. She tipped the can over, and the raccoon hurried into the woods. I learned that I could be a hero!

Publish ▸ **Share your narrative.**

After Reading

Show your understanding by talking about these questions with a partner.

1. What experience is Kelsey writing about?
2. How are Kelsey and her parents alike? How are they different?
3. How is Kelsey a hero?

ELPS 2G, 2H, 2I, 3E, 3I

Oral Language: Narrative Writing

The people who listen to you or read your writing are your audience. When you write or speak, use words your audience will understand.

Try IT Read the situation below. Then choose two audiences from the bottom of the page. Discuss with a partner how your narrative might be different for each audience.

Situation

You and your friends found something very interesting in the park. Narrate a story about it. Tell about what you found, how you found it, and how you felt.

Audiences

- Your babysitter
- Your school principal
- A pen pal in another country

Effective Talk

Answers to questions can be short or long. Including details in an answer helps your audience better understand you. The question below is answered three ways. The answer with the most details is the most complete.

What did you find outside?

bug

I found a bug.

I found a very strange bug in the park. I was playing catch, and the bug landed on my nose! I was so surprised that I sneezed!

Try IT Narrate a story about a time you found something interesting. Tell the events that happened. Include details about where you were, who you were with, and how you felt.

ELPS 2G, 2I, 3E, 3H

Language of Expository Writing

Expository writing is writing that explains. Expository writing has a beginning, middle, and ending. One kind of expository writing is a letter that explains how to do something.

Expository Letter Organization

Beginning
Middle
Ending

The beginning tells what the activity is and what supplies you will need.

The middle tells how to do the activity. It explains each step in order.

The ending tells why you like the activity.

Turn and Talk

Explain how to play your favorite game.

To play _____, you _____.

Vocabulary: Expository Writing

expository	**explain**	**information**
detail	**directions**	**chronological**

1. **Say the word.** Listen as your teacher reads the words aloud. Then repeat each word. Some vowels make the long *a* sound like *ai* in *rain* and *sail*. Which words have the long *a* sound. Pronounce these words with a partner.

2. **Discover the meaning.** Work with a partner to write a sentence using each vocabulary word that you know.

3. **Learn more.** Listen as your teacher explains the meaning of each word. Retell the word meanings to a partner. Then write sentences using the words you did not know.

4. **Show your understanding.** Listen as your teacher reads the question below. Answer the question in your notebook.
   - What kinds of details belong in expository writing?

5. **Write it, show it.** In your notebook, add pictures, words, and sentences to help you remember the vocabulary words.

Reading the Expository Model

What Do You Know?

Next you will read Maria's expository letter on page 128 about how to grow a flower. Do you know how to grow a flower? What steps would you follow?

Listening

Listen as your teacher or a classmate reads Maria's letter aloud. As you listen, write notes about Maria's directions. Then discuss the questions below with a partner.

1. What is Maria explaining?
2. What steps must you follow to grow a flower?
3. Explain why Maria wrote this letter.

Key How-To Words

then	first	next
soon	finally	when

Look at the words in the box. Listen as your teacher reads them aloud. Find the words in the letter on page 128. Notice the order of the words. Then use one or more of the words to write a sentence.

Read Along

Now it's your turn to read. Turn to page 128. As your teacher reads aloud, follow along in your book.

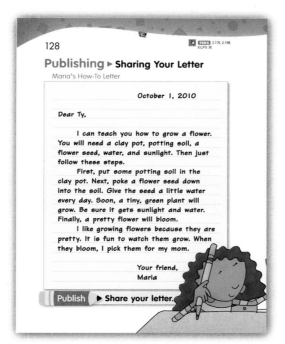

128

TEKS 2.17E, 2.19B
ELPS 3E

Publishing ▶ **Sharing Your Letter**

Maria's How-To Letter

October 1, 2010

Dear Ty,

I can teach you how to grow a flower. You will need a clay pot, potting soil, a flower seed, water, and sunlight. Then just follow these steps.

First, put some potting soil in the clay pot. Next, poke a flower seed down into the soil. Give the seed a little water every day. Soon, a tiny, green plant will grow. Be sure it gets sunlight and water. Finally, a pretty flower will bloom.

I like growing flowers because they are pretty. It is fun to watch them grow. When they bloom, I pick them for my mom.

Your friend,
Maria

Publish ▶ Share your letter.

After Reading

When you summarize, you briefly tell the main ideas. Summarize the letter to a partner. Then listen to your partner's summary.

⭐ ELPS 2G, 2H, 2I, 3E, 3I

Oral Language: Expository Writing

The people who listen to you or read your writing are your audience. When you write or speak, use language your audience will understand.

Try IT Read the situation below. Then choose two audiences from the bottom of the page. Discuss with a partner how your explanation might be different for each audience.

Situation

You love art projects. You want to teach others how to make art. Explain how to make a paper collage.

Audiences

- Students in your art class
- Your five-year-old brother
- A grandparent in another town

Effective Talk

Answers to questions can be short or long. Including details in an answer helps your audience better understand you. The question below is answered three ways. The answer with the most details is the most complete.

How do you make a paper collage?

magazines

▽

First, gather magazines.

▽

To make a collage, first gather magazines. The pages should have pictures that you can cut out.

Try IT Explain to a partner how to make an art project. Include details to make your ideas easy to follow.

ELPS 2G, 2I, 3E, 3G, 3H

Language of Persuasive Writing

Persuasive writing is writing that tries to get its readers to think or act a certain way. It has a beginning, middle, and ending. A persuasive letter is one kind of persuasive writing.

Persuasive Letter Organization

Beginning

Middle

Ending

> **The beginning states your opinion.**

> **The middle explains your reasons.**

> **The ending asks the reader to do something.**

Turn and Talk

What do you think should change in your school? Persuade a partner to share your opinion.

Our school should _____.

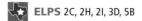
Vocabulary: Persuasive Writing

persuasive	**persuade**	**convince**
opinion	**reason**	**community**

1. **Say the word.** Listen as your teacher reads the words aloud. Then repeat each word.

2. **Discover the meaning.** In your notebook, write the words you know and their meanings. Then discuss examples of those words with a partner. For example, one *reason* to wear a bike helmet is to stay safe.

3. **Learn more.** Listen as your teacher explains the meaning of each word. Retell the word meanings to a partner. Then write each word and its meaning in your notebook.

4. **Show your understanding.** Listen as your teacher reads the questions below. Answer them in your notebook.
   - Can you prove an opinion?
   - When have you tried to convince someone? What reasons did you give?

5. **Write it, show it.** Add words, drawings, and sentences to your notebook to help you remember the vocabulary words.

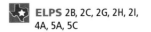 ELPS 2B, 2C, 2G, 2H, 2I, 4A, 5A, 5C

Reading the Persuasive Model

What Do You Know?

Next you will read Conall's persuasive letter on page 171 about washing your hands. When should you wash your hands? Why do you think washing your hands is important?

Listening

Listen as your teacher or a classmate reads Conall's persuasive letter aloud. As you listen, write down important details. Then discuss the questions below with a partner.

1. Why is Conall writing to his parents?
2. What reasons does Conall use to support his idea?

Key Persuasive Words

dear	should	your
they	keeps	sincerely

Look at the words in the box. Listen as your teacher reads them aloud. Notice the vowels *ea* in *dear* and *ee* in *keeps*. Both sets of vowels make the long *e* sound. Sound out the words. Then write them in your notebook.

Read Along

Now it's your turn to read. Turn to page 171. As your teacher reads aloud, follow along in your book.

TEKS 2.17E, 2.20
ELPS 2I, 3E

Persuasive Letter **171**

Conall's Persuasive Letter

March 18, 2011

Dear Mom and Dad,

You should remember to wash your hands. Germs live on your skin. They even hide.

Scrub your hands with soap and water. It stops germs from spreading. Washing hands keeps your food safer, too. Best of all, it keeps you from getting sick.

You can make our home a healthier place. Send those germs down the drain. Wash your hands!

Sincerely,
Conall

Publish ▶ Share your letter.

1. Write a neat copy of your letter.
2. Read the final copy before you share it.

After Reading

You can tell that Conall cares about health, even though he does not use those exact words. Explain to a partner how you know.

ELPS 2G, 2H, 2I, 3E, 3I

Oral Language: Persuasive Writing

The people who listen to you or read your writing are your audience. When you write or speak, use language your audience will understand.

Try It Read about the situation below. Then choose two audiences from the bottom of the page. Discuss with a partner how you might persuade each audience differently.

Situation

Your favorite show is on television. The person you are watching TV with wants to watch something else. Convince this person to watch your show instead.

Audiences

- Your mother
- Your school librarian
- A friend visiting from out of town

Effective Talk

Answers to questions can be short or long. Including details in an answer helps your audience better understand you. The question below is answered three ways. The answer with the most details is the most complete.

Why should I watch your show?

funny

▽

My show is funny.

▽

You should watch my show because the characters are very funny. They have silly adventures that will make you laugh.

Try IT Your opinion is what you think or believe about something. Persuade a partner to share your opinion about your favorite television show. Give reasons why you think your partner will like it.

ELPS 2G, 2I, 3E, 3G

Language of Response Writing

Response writing is writing that tells about texts you have read. It is a way to share your ideas with other readers. Book reviews and comparison essays are two kinds of response writing. A response to a text always has a beginning, middle, and ending.

Beginning

Middle

Ending

Book Review Organization

The beginning tells about the book.

The middle tells about your favorite part.

The ending explains why other people should read this book.

Turn and Talk

What book do you think your class would like to read? Why?

My class would like _____ because _____.

Vocabulary: Response to Texts

response	literature	informational
fiction	nonfiction	compare

1) **Say the word.** Listen as your teacher reads the words aloud. Then repeat each word.

2) **Discover the meaning.** Work with a partner to write sentences using the words you know.

3) **Learn more.** Listen as your teacher explains the meaning of each word. Retell the word meanings to a partner. Then write sentences using the words you did not know.

4) **Show your understanding.** Listen as your teacher reads the questions below. Answer them in your notebook.
- What is your favorite kind of literature?
- What is one informational text that you have read?
- Is a book about plants probably fiction or nonfiction? Why?

5) **Write it, show it.** Include drawings or notes in your notebook to help you remember the meanings of the vocabulary words.

ELPS 2B, 2C, 2G, 2H, 2I, 4A, 5A, 5B, 5C

Reading the Response Model

What Do You Know?

Next you will read "The Great Nate," a book review on page 198 about the book *Nate the Great, San Francisco Detective*. Have you ever read this book? Does it sound like a book you might enjoy?

Listening

Listen as your teacher or a classmate reads "The Great Nate" aloud. As you listen, write notes about the book. Then discuss the questions below with a partner.

1. What is *Nate the Great, San Francisco Detective* about?
2. What does Nate find in the messy bag?
3. Who do you think would like the book?

Key Response Words

great	written	story
lost	best	worse

Look at the words in the box. Listen as your teacher reads them aloud. Notice the consonant blend *st* at the end of *best* and *lost*. Sound out the words. Then write a sentence using *best* and *lost*.

Read Along

Now it's your turn to read. Turn to page 198. As your teacher reads aloud, read along in your book.

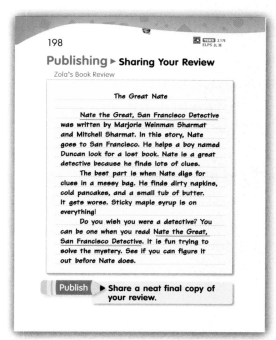

After Reading

Show your understanding by talking about these questions with a partner.

1. Do you want to read *Nate the Great, San Francisco Detective*? Why or why not?

2. How did reading the book review help you understand the story?

ELPS 2G, 2H, 2I, 3E, 3I

Oral Language: Response to Texts

The people who listen to you or read your writing are your audience. When you write or speak, use language your audience will understand.

Try It Read the situation below. Then choose two audiences from the bottom of the page. Discuss with a partner how your response might be different for each audience.

Situation

You received a book as a present from a friend. You enjoyed it so much that you want to talk about it with everyone. Share what the book is about, the best part, and why your audience would like it.

Audiences

- A child in kindergarten
- A teenage neighbor
- Your best friend

Effective Talk

Answers to questions can be short or long. Including details in an answer helps your audience better understand you. The question below is answered three ways. The answer with the most details is the most complete.

Why will I enjoy this book?

nature

▽

It teaches about nature.

▽

People who like nature will love this book. It teaches all about different plants and animals in Texas.

Try It Choose a book that you and your partner have read. Explain your opinion about the book. Did you like it? Why or why not? Then discuss your partner's opinion. How do your opinions compare?

ELPS 2G, 2I, 3E

Language of Creative Writing

Creative writing is writing that comes from your imagination. Stories, plays, and poems are all kinds of creative writing. Stories always have a beginning, middle, and ending.

Story Organization

Beginning

Middle

Ending

The beginning names the main character, setting, and problem.

The middle develops the plot, or action, of the story.

The ending tells how the problem is finally solved.

Turn and Talk

Share what happened in the first story you ever read.

In the first story I ever read, _____.

Vocabulary: Creative Writing

creative	imagination	character
story	play	poem

1. **Say the word.** Listen as your teacher reads the words aloud. Then repeat each word.

2. **Discover the meaning.** With a partner, make a T-chart. Write all of the vocabulary words in one column. Write what you think they mean in the other column.

3. **Learn more.** Listen as your teacher explains the meaning of each word. Retell the word meanings to a partner. Then work with your partner to change or add to your chart.

4. **Show your understanding.** Listen as your teacher reads the questions below. Answer them in your notebook.
   - What type of creative writing do you most enjoy?
   - How are a story and a play alike? How are they different?

5. **Write it, show it.** Add words or drawings to your notebook to help you remember the meanings of the vocabulary words.

 ELPS 2B, 2C, 2G, 2H, 2I, 4A, 5B, 5C

Reading the Creative Model

What Do You Know?

Next you will read "Rabbit's Big Mistake," a story on page 240 about a rabbit who loves to dig holes. What do you think Rabbit's mistake might be? Do you think he will solve it?

Listening

Listen as your teacher or a classmate reads "Rabbit's Big Mistake" aloud. As you listen, write down things you notice about Rabbit. Then discuss the questions below with a partner.

1. How do the animals try to help Rabbit?
2. What pattern do you notice in this story?
3. What lesson does Rabbit learn?

Key Creative Writing Words

mistake	problem	cried
said	know	again

Look at the words in the box. Listen as your teacher reads them aloud. Notice that the letter *k* in the word *know* is silent. Sound out the words. Then write a sentence with the word *know*.

Read Along

Now it's your turn to read. Turn to page 240. As your teacher reads aloud, follow along in your book.

After Reading

You can show that you understood what you read by retelling the story. Retell "Rabbit's Big Mistake" to a partner using your own words. Then listen to your partner's retelling.

⭐ ELPS 2G, 2H, 2I, 3E, 3H, 3I

Oral Language: Creative Writing

The people who listen to you or read your writing are your audience. When you write or speak, use language your audience will understand.

Try It Read about the situation below. Then choose two audiences from the bottom of the page. Discuss with a partner how your play might be different for each audience.

Situation

You found some fun costumes at your school. You decide to create a play to perform with your friends. Narrate the play by telling what happens.

Audiences

- Your class
- Your parents
- A group of four-year-old children

Effective Talk

Answers to questions can be short or long. Including details in an answer helps your audience better understand you. The question below is answered three ways. The answer with the most details is the most complete.

What happens in the play?

> **rabbit finds**

▽

> A rabbit finds carrots.

▽

> A little rabbit goes on a search for food. He finds a huge bunch of carrots and decides to make soup for all his friends.

Try IT To narrate means to tell what happens. Tell a partner what happens in your play. Be sure to tell who the characters are and where the setting is.

 ELPS 2G, 2I, 3E

Language of Report Writing

A research report is a type of informational text. It shares what you learned about a topic. A report has a beginning, middle, and ending.

Report Organization

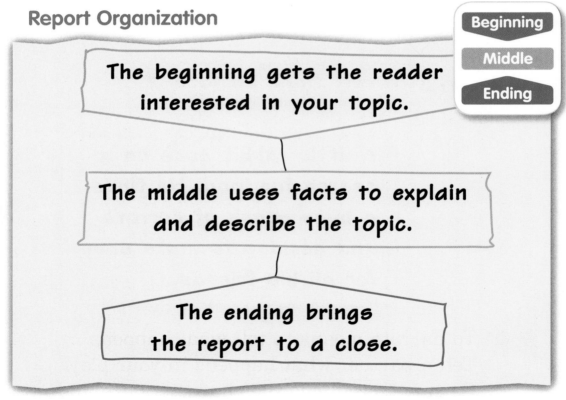

Beginning
Middle
Ending

The beginning gets the reader interested in your topic.

The middle uses facts to explain and describe the topic.

The ending brings the report to a close.

 Turn and Talk

What is something you would like to know more about?

I would like to know about _____.

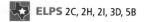
Vocabulary: Report Writing

research	source	evidence
reference	visuals	presentation

1. **Say the word.** Listen as your teacher reads the words aloud. Then repeat each word.

2. **Discover the meaning.** Work with a partner to brainstorm examples of each word you know. Make a word web using your examples.

3. **Learn more.** Listen as your teacher explains the meaning of each word. Retell the word meanings to a partner. Then add word webs to your notebook for the new words you learned.

4. **Show your understanding.** Listen as your teacher reads the questions below. Answer them in your notebook.
   - What do you do when you research?
   - What are some examples of sources?
   - Why is evidence important?

5. **Write it, show it.** Write the meaning of each vocabulary word in your notebook. Include pictures and words to help you remember what they mean.

 ELPS 2B, 2C, 2G, 2H, 2I, 4A, 5A, 5C

Reading the Report Model

What Do You Know?

Next you will read "Humming Wonders," a report on pages 287–289 about hummingbirds. What do you know about hummingbirds? Have you ever seen a hummingbird in real life?

Listening

Listen as your teacher or a classmate reads "Humming Wonders" aloud. As you listen, write down the main ideas. Then discuss the questions below with a partner.

1. What do hummingbirds look like?
2. What does a hummingbird eat?
3. Why did Tori write about hummingbirds?

Key Report Words

amazing	tiny	like
size	very	because

Look at the words in the box. Listen as your teacher reads them aloud. Notice the silent *e* at the end of the words *size* and *like*. The silent *e* makes both words have the long *i* sound. Sound out the words. Then write them in your notebook.

Read Along

Now it's your turn to read. Turn to pages 287–289. As your teacher reads aloud, follow along in your book.

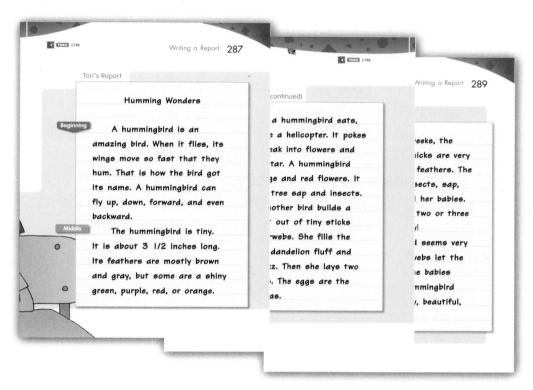

After Reading

When you summarize, you briefly tell the main ideas. Summarize "Humming Wonders" for a partner. Then listen to your partner's summary.

Oral Language: Report Writing

The people who listen to you or read your writing are your audience. When you write or speak, use language your audience will understand.

Try It Read about the situation below. Then choose two audiences from the bottom of the page. Discuss with a partner how your report might be different for each audience.

Situation

You visit a museum where you see a dinosaur skeleton. You are so amazed by it that you decide to learn more. You do some research. Share what you learned.

Audiences

- Your coach
- A classmate
- A cousin in preschool

Effective Talk

Answers to questions can be short or long. Including details in an answer helps your audience better understand you. The question below is answered three ways. The answer with the most details is the most complete.

What did dinosaurs eat?

food

▽

They ate plants and animals.

▽

Some dinosaurs ate other animals, but most dinosaurs ate plants. You can tell by looking at the dinosaurs' teeth.

Try IT What have you learned about dinosaurs from books, television, or the Internet? Describe a dinosaur you know to a partner. Share ideas about what it looked like, when it lived, and what it ate.

Reference Materials

Two kinds of reference materials can help you learn new words and use them correctly. They are a thesaurus and a dictionary. Let's find out how using these reference materials can make your writing even better!

Thesaurus

Different words that mean the same thing are called **synonyms**. A thesaurus lists synonyms for words. If you want to find another word for *turn*, you can look in a thesaurus. A thesaurus lists words in ABC order.

Owls *turn* **their heads to search for food.**

Thesaurus entry

turn   verb 1. The hands on the clock turn. *circle, spin, swivel*

Choosing a Synonym

You can use the synonym *swivel* instead of the word *turn*. *Swivel* is more specific and descriptive.

Owls *swivel* **their heads to search for food.**

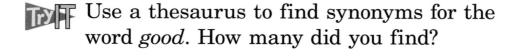 Use a thesaurus to find synonyms for the word *good*. How many did you find?

TEKS 2.25B
ELPS 4C

Dictionary

Dictionaries are found in the reference section. A dictionary tells you many things about words.

Guide Words
These words are found at the top of each page. They show the first and last entry words.

Entry Word
These are the words listed in ABC order on each page.

Spelling
Each entry word is spelled correctly.

Meaning
The meaning or meanings of each entry word are given.

Example Sentence
Each entry word is used in a sentence.

Some dictionaries show the pronunciation of a word.

ca • nar • y (kə **nâŕ** ē)

Sample Dictionary Page

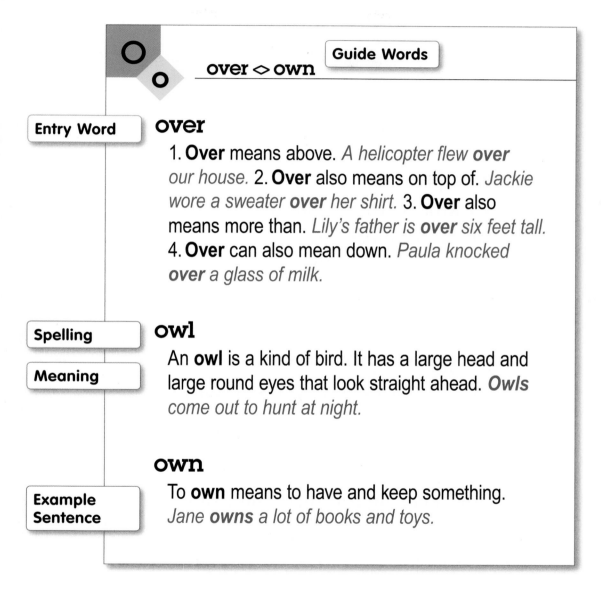

Guide Words

over ◇ own

Entry Word

over

1. **Over** means above. *A helicopter flew **over** our house.* 2. **Over** also means on top of. *Jackie wore a sweater **over** her shirt.* 3. **Over** also means more than. *Lily's father is **over** six feet tall.* 4. **Over** can also mean down. *Paula knocked **over** a glass of milk.*

Spelling

owl

Meaning

An **owl** is a kind of bird. It has a large head and large round eyes that look straight ahead. *Owls come out to hunt at night.*

own

Example Sentence

To **own** means to have and keep something. *Jane **owns** a lot of books and toys.*

 Ask a partner for directions for how to look up a word. Then follow your partner's directions step by step.

ELPS 2C, 3D, 3E, 4G

Basic Grammar and Writing

What's Ahead

Learning Language

Work with a partner. Read the meanings and share your answers.

1. A sentence is a group of words that expresses a complete thought.
   What are some parts of a sentence?
2. When you practice, you do something over and over again until you are good at it.
   What is something that you practice?
3. When something makes sense, you understand it.
   Tell about a time something didn't make sense to you.

Do you remember playing with blocks? Maybe you liked building forts or houses or towers. Words are just like building blocks, but instead of places, you build sentences. This section will help you use the best words in your sentences.

Working with Words

You already know many, many words, and you will learn many more as you read and study.

Words fit into different groups. Some words are nouns, some are pronouns, and so on. This chapter talks about nouns, pronouns, verbs, adjectives, and adverbs.

Mini Table of Contents

Annie

Learning About Nouns

A **noun** is a word that names a **person**, **place**, or **thing**.

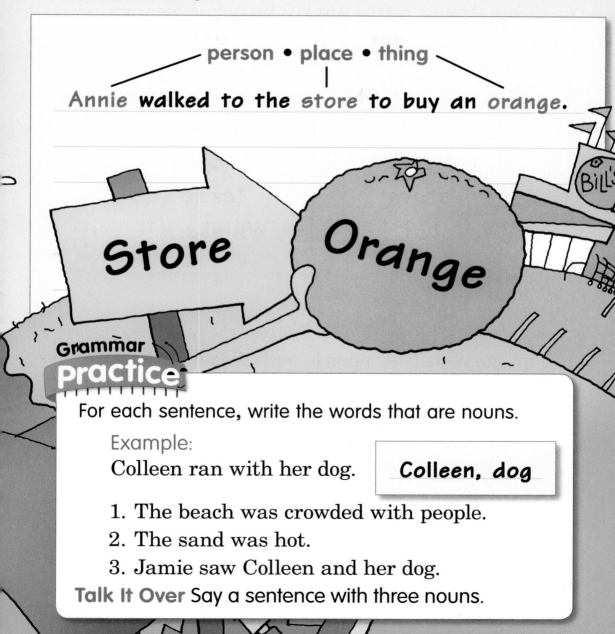

person • place • thing

Annie **walked to the** store **to buy an** orange.

Store

Orange

BILL'S

Grammar practice

For each sentence, write the words that are nouns.

Example:
Colleen ran with her dog. | **Colleen, dog**

1. The beach was crowded with people.
2. The sand was hot.
3. Jamie saw Colleen and her dog.

Talk It Over Say a sentence with three nouns.

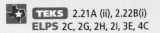
TEKS 2.21A (ii), 2.22B(i)
ELPS 2C, 2G, 2H, 2I, 3E, 4C

Common and Proper Nouns

A **common noun** names any person, place, or thing. A **proper noun** names a special person, place, or thing. Proper nouns always begin with capital letters.

Common Nouns	Proper Nouns
girl	Lina
street	Oak Street
state	Texas
cat	Whiskers

Grammar practice

Copy the underlined noun in each sentence below. Write **P** if it is a proper noun. Write **C** if it is a common noun. Capitalize the proper nouns.

1. My cousin, <u>thomas</u>, lives there.
2. He plays the <u>violin</u>.
3. I played with his dog, <u>bowser</u>.
4. My <u>cousin</u> is coming here to visit.

Talk It Over Say a sentence with a common noun. Then say a sentence with a proper noun. Discuss with a partner how the two nouns are different.

Singular and Plural Nouns

Nouns can be singular or plural. **Singular** means *one*. **Plural** means *more than one*. To make most nouns plural, add **-s** at the end of the word.

Singular Nouns	Plural Nouns
coat	coats
rabbit	rabbits
girl	girls

Grammar practice

Copy the underlined noun in each sentence below. Write **S** if the noun is singular and **PL** if it is plural.

1. They saw two new <u>bikes</u>.
2. Andi put on her <u>jacket</u>.
3. Mike quickly put on his <u>shoes</u>.

Talk It Over Say a sentence with the plural form of the word **book**.

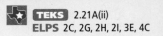 TEKS 2.21A(ii)
ELPS 2C, 2G, 2H, 2I, 3E, 4C

Nouns That End in -es

To form the plural of a noun that ends with **sh**, **ch**, **x**, **s**, and **z**, add **-es** to the end of the word.

Singular Nouns	Plural Nouns
wish	wishes
bunch	bunches
box	boxes
dress	dresses
buzz	buzzes

Grammar practice

Write the plural form for the underlined noun in each sentence below.

1. Dad made several <u>batch</u> of pancakes.
2. Grandma used two <u>mix</u> for the dip.
3. Gina picked <u>bunch</u> of violets.
4. Mom put them in tall <u>glass</u> on the table.

Talk It Over Say a sentence with the plural form of the word **lunch**.

Nouns That End in y

To form the plural of many nouns that end in **y**, remember this rule.

> Change the **y** to **i** and add **-es**.

lady ⟶ ladi + es = ladies

Singular Nouns	Plural Nouns
puppy	puppies
penny	pennies
jelly	jellies
story	stories

Grammar practice

Use the rule above to write the plural of each noun below. Then write a sentence using each plural noun.

1. party   2. pony   3. baby   4. city

Talk It Over Say a sentence with the plural form of the word **country**.

Possessive Nouns

A **possessive noun** shows ownership. To make a singular noun possessive, place an **'s** at the end of the word. To form most plural possessives, add the apostrophe **'** at the end of the word.

Have you seen Bobbi's hamster?

> The hamster belongs to Bobbi.

We saw the rabbits' tracks.

> The tracks belong to more than one rabbit.

Grammar practice

For each sentence, write the possessive noun.

Example:

Our neighbor's car is orange.　　**neighbor's**

1. Mr. Lee's dog is friendly.
2. That bicycle's tire is flat.
3. The school's doors were just painted.

Talk It Over Say a sentence with a possessive noun.

How can I use nouns?

Use **specific nouns** to give the reader a better picture of what you mean. If you use the word *flower*, it means any flower. But if you use the word *tulip*, your reader knows exactly what you mean.

General Nouns	Specific Nouns
neighbor	Mr. Cosfa
park	Central Park
building	firehouse
dog	terrier
tree	maple

Grammar practice

For each general noun below, write a specific noun.

Example:
teacher   **Ms. Daniels**

1. show   2. ocean   3. friend
4. bird   5. snack   6. school

Talk It Over Say a sentence using a specific noun for the general noun **snack**.

 **TEKS** 2.21A(vi)
ELPS 2C, 2G, 2H, 2I, 3C, 3E, 4C, 5E

Using Pronouns

A **pronoun** is a word that takes the place of a noun. Here are some common pronouns.

I	**he**	**she**	**we**	**they**	**you**
me	**him**	**her**	**us**	**them**	**it**

Then Claudia and Stella jumped rope.

Look at how the pronoun they replaces the nouns in the sentence above.

Then they jumped rope.

Grammar practice

For each sentence, write the pronoun.

1. They see a deer cross the road.
2. "Does the deer see us?" asked Sam.
3. Then the deer sees them.
4. The dog barks at it, and the deer runs.

Talk It Over Use pronouns to share a few sentences about a good friend.

Singular and Plural Pronouns

Pronouns are **singular** and **plural** just like nouns. Remember that singular means *one* and plural means *more than one*.

One

More Than One

Singular Pronouns   **Plural Pronouns**

I	she	we	us
me	he	they	them
it			

Grammar practice

Choose the correct pronoun to take the place of the underlined noun or nouns.

1. <u>Hanna and Kim</u> play. *(He, They)*
2. <u>The bird</u> flew to the feeder. *(We, It)*
3. Where was <u>Franco</u>? *(he, they)*
4. <u>Theresa</u> swims well. *(She, He)*

Talk It Over Use the pronoun **she** in a sentence. Then use the pronoun **them** in a sentence.

TEKS 2.21A(vi)
ELPS 2C, 2G, 2H, 2I, 3C, 3E, 4C, 5E

Using *I* and *Me*

When you write about yourself, use the singular pronoun **I** or **me**. The word **I** is always capitalized.

I always help my brother.

Tam and I are working together.

> Use **I** as a subject.

Fran gave me the letter.

Sandi told Mom and me about it.

> Use **me** after an action verb.

practice

Choose the correct pronoun for each sentence.

Example:

Lori asked *(I, me)* to go skating. | **me** |

1. *(I, me)* ran around the playground.
2. Jack and *(I, me)* played tag.
3. Dad asked *(I, me)* to clean my room.

Talk It Over Tell about your day using **I** and **me**.

Using *We* and *Us*

When you write about yourself and others, use the plural pronouns **we** and **us**.

We **are going to the school picnic.**

> Use **we** as the **subject** of a sentence.

Mr. Tylor asked us **a few questions.**

> Use **us** after an action verb.

Grammar Practice

Choose either **we** or **us** for each sentence below.

Example:

Please give _____ the invitations. | **us** |

1. _____ will plan the party together.
2. Mom and Dad always give _____ snacks.
3. _____ want to make the decorations.

Talk It Over Practice saying sentences with **we** or **us**.

 **TEKS** 2.21A(vi)
ELPS 2C, 2G, 2H, 2I, 3C, 3E, 4C, 5E

Possessive Pronouns

A **possessive pronoun** shows who or what owns something. It takes the place of a possessive noun.

| my | his | her | its | our | their |

Possessive Nouns	**Possessive Pronouns**
Devon's mitt	his mitt
Jenna's class	her class
Tom and Bina's pictures	their pictures
the book's cover	its cover

Grammar practice

Choose the correct pronoun for each underlined possessive noun below.

1. Did you find <u>Olivia's</u> locket? *(her, its)*
2. Mom saw <u>Leon's</u> hat. *(her, his)*
3. This is <u>Jake and Ron's</u> room. *(their, his)*
4. We fixed the <u>bike's</u> tire. *(its, his)*

Talk It Over Use possessive nouns to talk about something special that you or a friend owns.

How can I use pronouns?

Pronouns can be used to form contractions. A **contraction** is a shortened word made from two words.

Pronoun + Verb = Contraction

he	+ is	=	he's
she	+ is	=	she's
it	+ is	=	it's
you	+ are	=	you're
we	+ are	=	we're
they	+ are	=	they're

An apostrophe (**'**) shows that one or more letters are left out.

Grammar Practice

Write the contraction for each set of words in the sentences below.

1. I think *(it is)* almost time to go home.
2. Coach Lee says *(you are)* a good pitcher.
3. *(He is)* our neighbor.
4. Mom said *(we are)* going on a trip!

Talk It Over Tell about somewhere exciting you have gone using at least three contractions.

TEKS 2.21A(i)
ELPS 2C, 2G, 2H, 2I, 3E, 4C

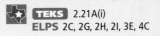

Learning About Verbs

There are three main types of verbs: action verbs, helping verbs, and linking verbs.

Action Verbs

An **action verb** tells what action is being done.

> **The kangaroo** hops.
>
> **My puppy** jumps.
>
> **Our friend Lin** sings.

Grammar practice

Write the action verb from each sentence below.

Example:

We clean our desks.　　| **clean** |

1. The rain pounds the sidewalk.
2. Little frogs leap in the grass.
3. The trees bend in the wind.

Talk It Over Use action verbs to tell about activities that your class does.

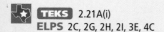
Helping Verbs

Sometimes a verb has more than one word. It has a main verb that shows action and a helping verb. A helping verb comes before the main verb. It helps to show action or time. Here are examples.

| am | is | are | was | were | will |

We were reading stories.

The helping verb **were** helps the main verb **reading**.

Grammar practice

Write the helping verb and the main verb from each sentence below.

Example:

I am playing at Katie's house. | **am playing** |

1. We were making a scrapbook.
2. I am finding pictures for the pages.
3. Katie was looking for decorations.

Talk It Over Use three helping verbs to talk about something that you enjoy doing.

Linking Verbs

Linking verbs complete a thought by linking two ideas in a sentence. The following *be* verbs can be linking verbs. (Most linking verbs can also be used as helping verbs. See page 399.)

am	is	are	was	were

I **am** hungry.

My cat **is** very pretty.

Sam and Dana **are** friends.

Lani **was** a funny girl.

We **were** lost.

Grammar practice

Write a sentence for each of the linking verbs below. Underline the linking verbs in your sentences.

Example:
were

> We <u>were</u> late for school.

1. am   2. are   3. were   4. is

Talk It Over Say a sentence using the linking verb **is**.

Verb Tenses

The tense of a verb tells when the action happens. The action can happen in the **present**, in the **past**, or in the **future**.

Present Tense The action is happening.

> Andy skates with his friends.

Past Tense The action did happen.

> Andy skated yesterday.

Future Tense The action will happen.

> Andy will skate tomorrow.

Grammar practice

Write a sentence for each of the verbs below. Then tell the tense of each verb.

1. plays
2. dropped
3. talked
4. will bake
5. reads

Talk It Over Discuss what you did yesterday, what you are doing now, and what you will do tomorrow.

TEKS 2.21B
ELPS 2C, 2G, 2H, 2I, 3E, 4C, 5D

How can I use verbs with subject nouns?

A verb will be correct if it **agrees in number** with its subject noun. That means a singular subject needs a singular verb, and a plural subject needs a plural verb.

Singular Subject Noun	Singular Verb

Juan laughs.

Dad cleans.

Sue dives.

Plural Subject Noun	Plural Verb

The boys laugh.

We clean.

Kim and I dive.

Grammar practice

For each sentence below, write the verb that agrees with the subject.

1. The children (*draw, draws*) pictures.
2. Gabe (*buy, buys*) a comic book.
3. Jon (*ride, rides*) his bike after school.
4. My friends (*play, plays*) chess.

Talk It Over Use the verb **laugh** and a subject noun in a sentence. Make sure that the subject noun you choose agrees with the verb.

How can I use verbs correctly with subject pronouns?

Your verb will be correct if it **agrees in number** with its subject pronoun. Look at the chart below.

Singular Subject Pronoun	Singular Verb	Plural Subject Pronoun	Plural Verb
He	likes snow.	They	like snow.
She	wants help.	We	want help.
It	drinks water.	They	drink water.

Grammar practice

For each sentence below, write the verb that agrees with the subject.

1. They (*find, finds*) a lost dog.
2. It (*wag, wags*) its tail!
3. She (*want, wants*) to find the owners.
4. He (*is, are*) happy to see Spot again.

Talk It Over Use the verb **goes** and a subject pronoun in a sentence. Make sure that the subject pronoun you choose agrees with the verb.

 TEKS 2.21A(iii)
ELPS 2C, 2G, 2H, 2I, 3B, 3E, 4C

Working with Adjectives

An **adjective** is a word that describes a noun. Adjectives help you add details to your writing.

Adjectives tell what kind.

Adjectives that tell **what kind** make writing fun to read.

The huge owl flew away.
The dog chased the yellow ball.

Grammar practice

For each sentence below, find the adjective that tells what kind.

Example:
Let's visit the brick building.

> brick

1. The building has a round dome.
2. A squeaky fan cools me.
3. I ate a spicy burrito.

Talk It Over Use three adjectives to tell what kind of books you like to read.

Adjectives tell which one.

Adjectives that tell **which one** make your writing clear. Here are some examples.

> this that those these

This book is very exciting.

I want to read that book again.

Did you hear those stories?

These pictures are my favorite.

 Grammar
Practice

For each sentence below, find the adjective that tells which one.

Example:

This book shows men on the moon. | This |

1. Grandpa remembers that day.
2. Those astronauts were brave.
3. Grandpa gave me these pictures.

Talk It Over Share about something in the classroom using adjectives that tell which one.

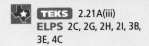

TEKS 2.21A(iii)
ELPS 2C, 2G, 2H, 2I, 3B, 3E, 4C

Adjectives tell how many.

Some adjectives tell you **how many.**

one **tree**	three **tickets**
two **pages**	four **birds**

Grammar practice

Write a sentence for each adjective below.

　　1. two　　2. three　　3. four　　4. five

Talk It Over Use a complete sentence to tell how many people you have in your family.

Articles

A, an, and *the* are special adjectives called **articles.** Use *a* before words that begin with a consonant. Use *an* before words that begin with a vowel.

a **lamb**	an **octopus**	the **zoo**

Grammar practice

Write one sentence using **a,** one sentence using **an,** and one sentence using **the.**

How can I use adjectives?

You can use adjectives to **compare** two people, places, or things.

Our car is smaller than your car.

> To compare **two** nouns, add **-er** to the end of the adjective.

The red car is the smallest one of all.

> To compare **three** or *more* nouns, add **-est** to the end of the adjective.

Grammar Practice

In each sentence below, choose the correct adjective.

1. He is the *(younger, youngest)* boy in class.
2. Danni is a *(faster, fastest)* runner than I am.
3. She is the *(taller, tallest)* girl I know.
4. Your chair is *(softer, softest)* than mine.

Talk It Over Compare objects in the classroom using adjectives.

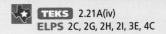 **TEKS** 2.21A(iv)
ELPS 2C, 2G, 2H, 2I, 3E, 4C

Learning About Adverbs

An **adverb** is a word that describes a verb. It answers **when**, **where**, or **how** an action happens.

> **It rained** yesterday. (When?)
> **We ran** inside. (Where?)
> **The thunder rumbled** loudly. (How?)

Grammar  practice

For each sentence below, write the adverb that answers the asking word in parentheses.

Example:
Mom and I went fishing today.
(When?)

> **today**

1. We sat quietly. *(How?)*
2. I let my bait sink down. *(Where?)*
3. A fish finally grabbed the bait. *(When?)*

Talk It Over Use adverbs to tell how, when, and where you like to eat lunch.

How can I use adverbs?

Using adverbs helps to make your writing clear. The adverbs in the following sentences answer **how**.

How?

Roy slowly poured the water.

Maria proudly read her report.

The snow fell softly.

Grammar practice

Write each sentence below, using the adverb in parentheses that you like best.

1. Otters swim *(smoothly, gracefully)*.
2. Prairie dogs *(quickly, always)* pop out of their holes.
3. Monkeys *(carefully, cleverly)* peel bananas.
4. Woodpeckers *(noisily, nervously)* peck trees.

Talk It Over Use adverbs to tell how you should act on the playground at recess.

Building Sentences

Sentences come in all sizes. Some are very long. Others are quite short. Every sentence must tell a complete thought. It must also begin with a capital letter and end with a punctuation mark. In this chapter, you will learn all about sentences.

Mini Table of Contents

Writing Complete Sentences

Correct Word Order

The words in a sentence must be in the correct order to make sense. The first group of words below does not make sense.

hamburger Billy eats a lunch for

If you put these words in the correct order, they tell a complete, clear sentence.

Billy eats a hamburger for lunch.

practice

Put the groups of words below in the correct order to make sentences.

Example:
is hamburger the hot.   **The hamburger is hot.**

1. pickles puts hamburger on his Billy
2. squirts his on ketchup hamburger he
3. a little likes also he mustard

Subject of a Sentence

The **naming part** of a sentence is called the **subject**. The subject tells who or what the sentence is about.

Ms. Davis **is our teacher.**

She **walks to school.**

Ms. Davis is the **subject** of the first sentence.
She is the **subject** of the second sentence.

Write the subject of each sentence below.

Example:
The school is near our teacher's house.

The school

1. The house has a big porch.
2. Students walk past her house.
3. Parents wave to Ms. Davis.

Talk It Over Say two sentences about school and then identify the subject of each sentence.

Predicate of a Sentence

The **telling part** of a sentence is called the **predicate**. It tells what the subject does. The predicate always includes a main verb.

> **Crickets** chirp loudly.

Chirp loudly is the predicate. It tells what the crickets do. The word **chirp** is the main verb.

practice

Write the predicate of each sentence below.

Example:
Crickets look like grasshoppers.

> **look like grasshoppers**

1. Many crickets hide during the day.
2. Crickets live on trees.
3. They move slowly in cold weather.

Talk It Over Say two sentences about an insect and then identify the predicate of each sentence.

Fixing Sentence Problems

Sentence Fragments

Every sentence needs a subject and a predicate to make sense. A **sentence fragment** is missing a subject or a predicate (verb).

Fragments	Sentences
Sleeps under a tree. (A subject is missing.)	**The dog sleeps under a tree.** (A subject is added.)
The dog in the yard. (A verb is missing.)	**The dog runs in the yard.** (A verb is added.)

 **practice**

The sentence fragments below are missing a subject or a verb. Make each one a sentence.

Example:
Ranger loudly. | **Ranger barks loudly.** |

1. plays in the park.
2. Ranger into the pond.
3. Chased me.
4. Water all over.

Rambling Sentences

A **rambling sentence** is one that goes on and on and on.

Rambling Sentence

> My mother told me to get some skim milk and I went to the cooler and I looked for a carton and I finally found it.

Try not to use the word **and** too many times.

Better Sentences

> My mother told me to get some skim milk. I went to the cooler and looked for a carton. I finally found it.

Rewrite this rambling sentence. Turn it into three or four sentences by taking out some of the *and's*.

Joanie calls her friends and she asks them to go to the park and they have fun swinging and they have fun sliding.

Subject-Verb Agreement

Subjects and verbs must agree in number. A singular subject must have a singular verb. A plural subject must have a plural verb.

Bob **has** *a silver wheelchair.*

> The **subject** and the **verb** are singular.

Two other boys have red wheelchairs.

> The **subject** and the **verb** are plural.

---

practice

Write the verb that agrees with the subject for each sentence below.

1. Justin *(push, pushes)* Bob's wheelchair.
2. Justin and Bob *(is, are)* good friends.
3. Bob *(tell, tells)* funny stories.
4. His friends always *(laugh, laughs)*.

Talk It Over Talk about what you like to do with your friends. Make sure that you use correct subject-verb agreement.

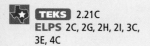
Using Different Kinds of Sentences

A **telling sentence** makes a statement.

You have a box of crayons.

An **asking sentence** asks a question.

Do you have a red crayon?

A **command sentence** gives directions or makes a request.

Put your crayons away.

An **exclamatory sentence** shows surprise or strong feelings.

Your crayons are going to fall!

 **practice**

Write what kind of sentence each one is.

1. How many crayons do you have?
2. I love your drawing!
3. Pass me the blue crayon.
4. I want to draw the ocean.

Talk It Over Use each kind of sentence to talk about something in your classroom.

TEKS 2.21B
ELPS 2C, 2G, 2H, 2I, 3C, 3E, 4C, 5D, 5F

Combining Short Sentences

Sometimes, short sentences have the same subject. These sentences can be combined to make longer sentences.

Short Sentences with the Same Subject

Jerry gets dressed. Jerry eats breakfast.

Combined Sentences

Jerry gets dressed and eats breakfast.

Combine these sentences to make longer sentences. Make sure that you use correct subject-verb agreement.

1. The school bus stops.
   The school bus picks up three students.
2. Jenna's friends talk. Jenna's friends laugh.
3. Kenny sits at his desk. Kenny opens his book.

Talk It Over Say two sentences that have the same subject. Then combine the sentences into one longer sentence. Remember that your subject and verb must agree in number.

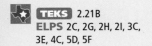
You can also combine short sentences that have the same predicate.

Short Sentences with the Same Predicate

Ellen cleaned the board.

Lila cleaned the board.

Combined Sentences

Ellen and Lila cleaned the board.

Combine these short sentences to make longer sentences. (You may need to change a singular verb to a plural verb in your new sentence. Your subject and verb must agree in number.)

1. Sharon jumps rope during recess.
   Jill jumps rope during recess.
2. Ryan learns about question marks.
   Thomas learns about question marks.
3. The girls like the goldfish.
   The boys like the goldfish.

Talk It Over Say two sentences that have the same predicate. Then combine the sentences into one longer sentence. Remember to use correct subject-verb agreement.

TEKS 2.17B
ELPS 2C, 4C

Writing Paragraphs

A paragraph is a group of sentences about the same topic. In a paragraph, you can describe something, give information, or tell how to do a task. Theo's paragraph on the next page tells about a hot-air balloon.

Mini Table of Contents

Theo's Paragraph

What I Saw

Topic Sentence

I saw a big hot-air balloon that looked like my sister's knee socks. It had bright blue and yellow stripes. A big basket with

Body Sentences

a man inside it hung under the balloon. The man shot spurts of fire into the balloon. Whoosh, whoosh! The flames made a loud sound. I waved to the man, and he waved back! It was the coolest

Closing Sentence

thing I have ever seen.

A paragraph has three main parts.

- The **topic sentence** tells what the paragraph is about. It states the main idea.
- The **body sentences** describe the topic.
- The **closing sentence** adds one last thought.

 **TEKS** 2.17B
ELPS 2C, 3E, 3G, 4C

Writing a Topic Sentence

The **topic sentence** names the topic or the main idea of the paragraph. Here are three ways to write a topic sentence.

1. **Asking a Question**

   Have you ever seen a hot-air balloon?

2. **Stating an Interesting Idea**

   Yesterday, a colorful hot-air balloon floated over my house.

3. **Making a Comparison**

   I saw a big hot-air balloon that looked like my sister's knee socks.

Talk it over.

Do you like Theo's choice for a topic sentence? Tell why or why not.

Writing Body Sentences

The **body sentences** of a paragraph share details about the topic. You can use details from a quick planning list to write the body sentences of your paragraph. Here's Theo's quick list.

Quick List

— blue and yellow stripes
— a big basket with a man in it
— fire shot into balloon
— a loud whoosh sound

Example Body Sentences

It had bright blue and yellow stripes.

A big basket with a man inside it hung under the balloon.

The man shot spurts of fire into the balloon.

TEKS 2.17B
ELPS 2C, 4C

Writing a Closing Sentence

A **closing sentence** says one last thing about your topic. Theo wrote his closing sentence in two different ways. Then he chose the one he liked best.

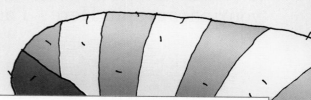

1. **Restating the Main Idea**

   Seeing the hot-air balloon was fun.

2. **Adding a Final Thought**

   It was the coolest thing I have ever seen.

practice

1. Write another ending sentence for Theo's paragraph.
2. Now write your own paragraph.

Indenting Each Paragraph

You **indent** a paragraph because it starts a new idea. *Indenting* means to begin writing farther in from the margin.

Example of Indenting

> The lion came close to the edge of its cage. It looked right at me. The lion growled, "Grrr!"
>
> Suddenly, Dad called me.

Talk it over.

Look at the writing below. What is the new idea in the second paragraph?

> I learned to swim! At first I was afraid of the water. Soon I was brave enough to swim in the deep water. Now swimming is my favorite thing to do.
>
> My little brother is learning to swim. I am helping him, but he is still a little afraid of the water. Today we will go swimming. I like swimming with my brother.

A Writer's Resource

Learning Language

Work with a partner. Read the meanings and share answers to the questions.

1. A **topic** is a subject of writing or speaking.
   What topics do you enjoy discussing?

2. A **graphic organizer** shows how words or ideas are connected.
   What are kinds of graphic organizers?

3. If you **get stuck**, you can't move further.
   When you get stuck on an assignment, what do you do?

4. A **resource** is something that can be used to help you find information.
   What resources have you used this week?

Sometimes you need help with your writing. Maybe you can't think of a good topic. Maybe you aren't sure how to gather details. Whenever you get stuck, turn to these pages for ideas and help.

How can I find a good topic?

Keep a writer's notebook.

Good writing ideas are everywhere. Keep a list of ideas in a notebook. Someday you may use these ideas in a story, a letter, a report, or even in a poem.

Write about what is going on around you.

You may see something interesting right in your own backyard. Ask open-ended questions about what you see to get more ideas to write about!

Sample Writer's Notebook

> A big gray squirrel is sitting on a
> bird feeder. How did it get up there? A
> red bird wants to come to the feeder.
> That squirrel is scaring the birds and
> throwing seeds all over! What will the
> birds do next?

Try It Ask open-ended questions about your neighborhood to get ideas for your writing.

List topics in your notebook.

List interesting people, places, and things in your writer's notebook. Then look over your lists when you need writing ideas.

Sample Writer's Notebook

People	Places	Things
teacher	school	car
pilot	home	bike
doctor	Ohio	lion
parent	library	desk
brother	zoo	game

Look for signs and labels.

Signs and labels can give lots of ideas for writing. Look for signs around your town and school. Notice food and clothing labels. Ask open-ended questions about why the signs and labels are there and what they mean. Then find sources to help you answer your questions.

Sample Writer's Notebook

The label on my red shirt says to wash with "like colors." What does "like colors" mean? Why should I follow the label's directions?

I asked my dad. He washes my laundry, so he should know. Dad said that I should wash my shirt with other red clothes. He reminded me of the time I washed my red sock with my white hat. My hat turned pink! Now I know why I should read the labels on my clothes!

Try It Choose a sign or label to write about. Ask two open-ended questions and then find the answers. You will have to decide which sources will help you get the information that you need.

Notice symbols and logos.

You can write about the symbols and logos around you. Symbols are pictures that have meaning. For example, the symbol for recycling is three arrows in the shape of a triangle. Logos are a type of symbol. They usually stand for a brand or company.

Sample Writer's Notebook

> Today at school I learned that the
>
> symbol for the Olympics is five rings of
>
> different colors on a white background.
>
> The five rings stand for the five
>
> continents that compete in the Olympic
>
> games. The rings are linked to show
>
> that people from around the world come
>
> together for the games.

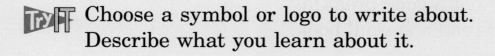 Choose a symbol or logo to write about. Describe what you learn about it.

How can I find special topics?

Review lists of topic ideas.

For **descriptive** writing, you could **describe** . . .
- a sister, a cousin, or a teacher. (People)
- your room, the school, or a library. (Places)
- a toy, a hat, a tree, or an octopus. (Things)

For **narrative** writing, you could **tell what happened** . . .
- during a ride on the bus.
- on your first day of school.
- in a funny dream.

For **expository** writing, you could **explain** . . .
- how to fly a kite.
- how to draw funny faces.
- information about eagles.

For **persuasive** writing, you could **convince** your reader to . . .
- be polite on a field trip.
- eat a good breakfast.
- read a special book.

How do I write topic sentences?

Know your purpose.

You write to describe, to share a story, to explain, or to convince someone. The reason for your writing is called your **purpose**. A topic sentence lets the reader know the main idea and purpose of a paragraph.

To Describe

Descriptive writing helps the reader see or hear a topic.

The red race car sounds like a jet plane.

To Share a Story

Narrative writing tells a story.

Yesterday, my brother broke his arm.

To Explain Something

Expository writing shares information.

Giving a dog a bath is a big job.

To Convince Someone

Persuasive writing tries to get the reader to agree with an opinion.

A turtle makes a great pet.

 TEKS 2.17B, 2.21A(vii)

How can I organize my ideas?

Use graphic organizers.

When you play softball, you follow a plan. First, you and your friends choose sides. Then you decide who bats first and so on. When you write, you also need a plan, and a graphic organizer can help. Look at the graphic organizer below and on pages 435–440.

List steps in a sequence chart.

Use a **sequence chart** to put details in order. Then follow the chart as you write.

Sample Sequence Chart

Topic	How to Bake Bread
First	Find the ingredients.
Next	Mix the ingredients.
Then	Turn on the oven.
Last	Bake the ingredients.

Compare topics with a Venn diagram.

Use a **Venn diagram** when you compare two topics. In spaces 1 and 2, list how the topics are different. In space 3, list how the topics are alike.

Sample Venn Diagram

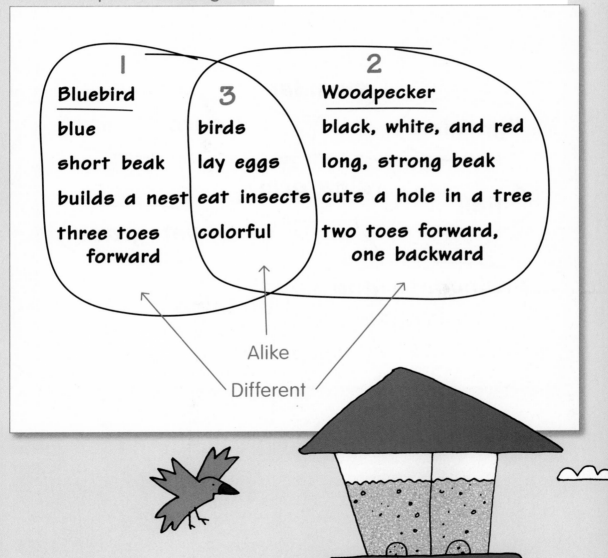

1 Bluebird	3	2 Woodpecker
blue	birds	black, white, and red
short beak	lay eggs	long, strong beak
builds a nest	eat insects	cuts a hole in a tree
three toes forward	colorful	two toes forward, one backward

Alike

Different

Gather details with a cluster.

Make a **cluster**, also called a **web**, about your topic. Write your topic in the middle of your paper. Draw a circle around it. Then write as many ideas as you can about your topic.

Sample Cluster

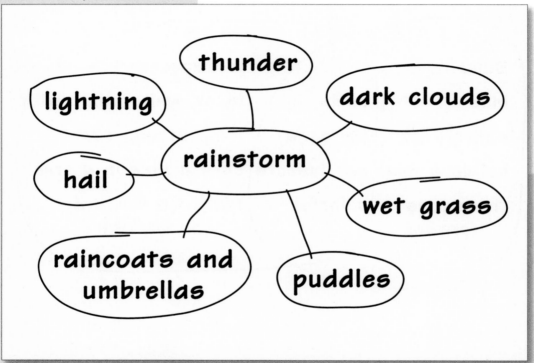

Gather details with a sensory chart.

Use a **sensory chart** to list different types of details for a topic. This chart is useful for writing poems.

Sample Sensory Chart

Topic: Lunch

Sight	Sound	Smell	Taste	Touch
bowl of tomato soup	spoons clinking on bowls	tomatoes	tomatoes	hot bowl
		cooked corn	salty crackers	cool milk
square crackers	crunching			dry crackers
	laughter	toasted bread	sweet corn	
glass of milk				soft, gooey cheese
			melted cheese	
grilled cheese sandwich				hot corn

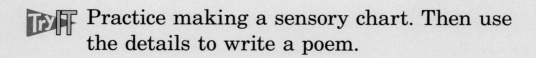 Practice making a sensory chart. Then use the details to write a poem.

Plan a story with a map.

Use a **story map** to help you remember important parts of a story. You can draw pictures or write words to make a story map.

Sample Story Map

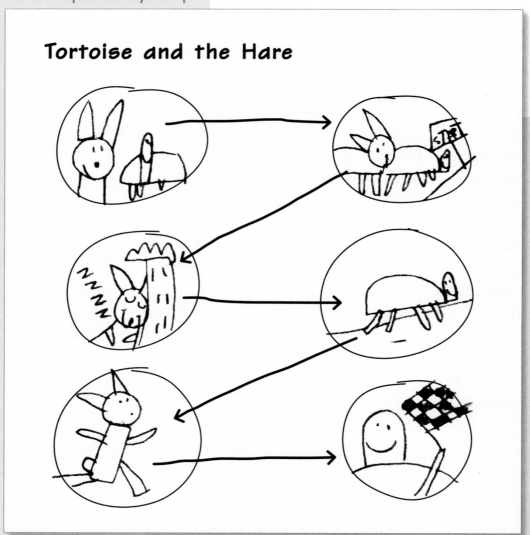

Tortoise and the Hare

Gather facts with a 5 W's chart.

Make a **5 W's chart** when you need to find important facts or details for your writing.

Sample 5 W's Chart

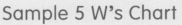

Who?	Mrs. Jones
What?	delivers the mail and small packages
When?	six days a week all year
Where?	to our apartment building
Why?	so we can read our mail it's her job

 TEKS 2.17B, 2.19B

Put events in order with a time line.

Make a **time line** to show when different events happened. A time line can use hours, days, months, or years. Time lines can help you plan your writing by putting events in chronological order.

Sample Time Line

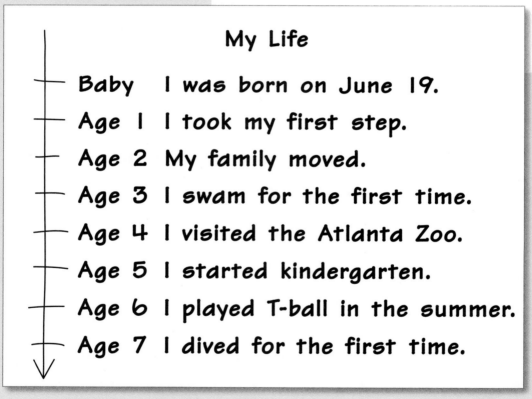

My Life

Baby   I was born on June 19.

Age 1   I took my first step.

Age 2   My family moved.

Age 3   I swam for the first time.

Age 4   I visited the Atlanta Zoo.

Age 5   I started kindergarten.

Age 6   I played T-ball in the summer.

Age 7   I dived for the first time.

Try It Practice using a time line. Record today's events and then use your time line to write a letter to a friend about your day. Be sure to use correct letter conventions.

How can I organize a letter?

Use the letter format.

Write letters that include the date, salutation, body text, and closing.

Put ideas in chronological order.

One way to organize ideas in a letter is to put them in **chronological order**. This means writing about events in the order that they happened.

Sample Letter

> July 14, 2011
>
> Dear Mom,
>
>   I am having a wonderful time at Grandma's house. Yesterday, we went to the movies. Then, we went shopping. Finally, we went swimming at the beach. I will write soon to tell you more!
>
>   Love,
>   Shauna

TEKS 2.19B

Put ideas in logical order.

Organize your ideas by writing them in an order that makes sense. You could describe a cause and its effect. You could tell about a problem and a solution. Writing your letter in a **logical order** makes it easier for your reader to understand.

Sample Letter

October 1, 2011

Dear Ms. Collier,

It takes a very long time to get through the lunch line at our school. Some kids don't get their lunches until lunchtime is almost over. Please add an extra lunch line in the cafeteria. The wait will be shorter, and kids will have time to enjoy their food.

Sincerely,

Josh

How should my writing voice change?

Match your voice with your purpose.

Whenever you write, keep your purpose in mind. Be sure to sound interested and confident in your topic, too.

Descriptive Voice

Use sensory details to describe a topic.

> My dad's match hit the newspaper. Pretty soon smoke came up from the pile of sticks. Then yellow and orange flames licked the wood. Sparks jumped through the grill over our campfire.

Narrative Voice

Write as if you were telling the story to a friend.

> I had to take care of Felix for two weeks. If you knew Felix, you would say, "Good luck!" He is a big, stubborn cat who loves to hide.

Expository Voice

Use specific details to explain your topic. Help your reader to understand information or to follow the steps.

> First, you spread glue where you want the glitter on your drawing. Next, sprinkle the glitter on the glue. Let it dry for a minute. Then shake the extra glitter off. Finally, let your picture dry completely.

Persuasive Voice

Use good reasons to help the reader decide to agree with you.

> When you go outside on a very cold day, be sure to wear a hat. You lose a lot of heat from the top of your head. A hat helps to keep your whole body warm.

How can I learn new words?

Keep a new-word notebook.

Keep a notebook for new words that you see and hear. Write each word and its meaning. Then write a sentence that uses that word. Add drawings.

Sample New Word Notebook

telescope (word)

an instrument used to look at stars (meaning)

Mara's family bought a telescope to look at the moon. (sentence)

truck (word)

a vehicle used to move large loads (meaning)

The truck delivered furniture to the house.

(sentence)

Use a dictionary.

You can learn what a word means by looking it up in a dictionary.

Sample Dictionary Entry

> **insect**   An insect is a small animal with six legs. A wasp is a flying insect. Some common insects are crickets, moths, and mosquitoes.

Sarah watches the red insect
cross the sidewalk.

Use a thesaurus.

A **thesaurus** is a book that lists words and their synonyms (words with the same meanings). Use a thesaurus to choose specific words.

Sample Thesaurus Entry

> **jacket**   *noun* coat, parka, windbreaker

Word Choice

General ▶ **Larry wore a** jacket **to the game.**

Specific ▶ **Larry wore a** parka **to the game.**

How can I connect my sentences?

Use time-order words.

Use **time-order words** to tell the order in which things happen or should be done.

Time-Order Word Chart

first	second	third
May 10	**May 11**	**May 12**
yesterday	today	tomorrow
then	now	later
first	next	last

Use prepositions.

Use **prepositions** to show location and order.

Prepositions Word Chart

above	**behind**	**near**
across	**below**	**on**
after	**beneath**	**outside**
against	**beside**	**over**
along	**between**	**through**
among	**beyond**	**toward**
around	**by**	**under**
at	**in**	**up**
before	**inside**	**within**

How can I make my report better?

Add a bar graph.

A **bar graph** helps the reader understand numbers you use in your writing. The bars compare two or more things. The graph below shows the number of library books read in three different classrooms during one month.

Sample Bar Graph

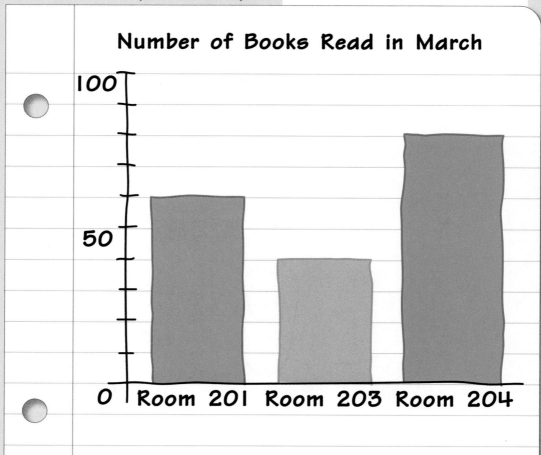

Number of Books Read in March

TEKS 2.25C, 2.27

Draw a diagram.

A **diagram** explains what something looks like or how it works so the reader can understand the information.

Sample Diagram

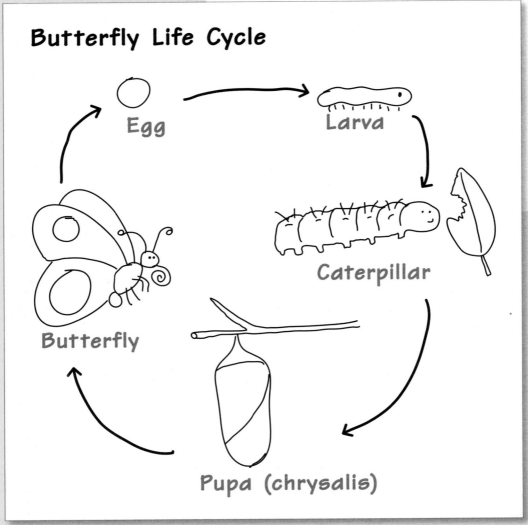

Butterfly Life Cycle

Egg

Larva

Caterpillar

Butterfly

Pupa (chrysalis)

Editing and Proofreading Marks

You can use the marks below when you revise and edit your writing. Your teacher may also use these marks to tell you how to improve your writing.

Symbol	Meaning	Example	Edited
≡	Capitalize a letter.	Jean Fritz wrote *George washington's Mother.*	Jean Fritz wrote *George Washington's Mother.*
/	Make a capital letter lowercase.	George's mother was Named Mary.	George's mother was named Mary.
⊙	Add a period.	Mary baked delicious gingerbread	Mary baked delicious gingerbread.
℘	Take something out.	Her son George he joined the army.	Her son George joined the army.
∧	Add a letter, a word, or words.	Mary wished her son would stay home.	Mary wished her son would stay home.
? ! , ∧ ∧ ∧	Insert punctuation.	In February of 1789 George was elected president.	In February of 1789, George was elected president.
sp. ◯	Correct the spelling error.	Mary wroot letters to her son.	Mary wrote letters to her son.
⌗	Start a new paragraph.	Mary liked writing and reading ⌗ One time she had . . .	Mary like writing and reading. One time she had . . .

Proofreader's Guide

Learning Language

Work with a partner. Read the meanings and share answers to the questions.

1. **Punctuation marks** separate words and letters so that writing makes sense.
   What punctuation marks do you use?

2. An **abbreviation** is a shortened word.
   What abbreviations do you know?

3. When you **pay attention**, you focus your thoughts or attention on something.
   When is it important to pay attention?

Checking
Mechanics

Rules help you in many ways. There are rules for keeping you safe. There are rules for playing games. There are also rules for writing. This chapter lists many rules for the **mechanics of writing**.

Rules for Punctuation

Punctuation marks are signals that help you understand writing. For example, a period tells you to stop at the end of a sentence. A comma tells you to pause. This chapter will explain these and other punctuation marks.

Use a Period

At the End of a Telling Sentence

George and Martha are silly.

After an Initial

S.E. Goode

D.L. Spruce

Susan B. Anthony

After an Abbreviation

Mr. Plant

Ms. Blossom

Dr. Gardener

Practice · Periods

Read the sentences below. Find where a period is missing. Write the word or letters that come before the missing period and then add the period.

Example: My teacher's name is Ms Potter.

> **Ms.**

1. Simon brings his lunch to school every day

2. His mother is Dr Brown.

3. She signs her name "Gina M Brown" on school forms.

4. Mr Brown is a carpenter.

5. Carpenters make things out of wood

6. Simon has a friend named T J Roberts.

Next Step: Write a sentence about your teacher. Include his or her name in your sentence.

TEKS 2.22C(i)
ELPS 2C, 3C, 4C

Use a Question Mark

After a Question

Who sat on my lunch?

Use an Exclamation Point

After a Sentence That Shows Strong Feeling

Uh-oh, there's a skunk on the playground!

After a Word That Shows Excitement

Wow!   Help!

 **practice**

Question Marks and Exclamation Points

Decide if each sentence below needs to end with a question mark or an exclamation point. Copy the sentences and end each with the correct punctuation mark.

Example: Hooray, the sun's coming out

> Hooray, the sun's coming out!

1. Is the storm over

2. Wow, that storm was bad

3. The wind blew so hard

4. Did the wind blow anything over

5. My bird feeder is missing

6. Was there any flooding

Learning Language: Write two sentences about a bad storm. Make one sentence a question and make the other show strong feelings. Then say two more sentences on the same topic to a partner. One sentence should be a question and the other should show excitement.

Use a Comma

A comma looks like a period with a tail on it (**,**).

Between Words in a Series

    I love red, purple, and silver.

In Compound Sentences

    Those colors are nice, but I like the color green best of all.

(In compound sentences, the comma is put in front of the conjunctions **and**, **but**, and **so**.)

To Help Set Off a Speaker's Words

    Russ said, "I love kickball!"

 **Commas 1**
- **Commas in a Series**
- **Commas in Compound Sentences**

For each sentence, write the word or words that should be followed by a comma. Write the comma, too.

Example: I see Canada Mexico and the United States on this globe.

> **Canada, Mexico,**

1. Juan has family in Ohio Utah and Florida.

2. Some kids in my class have been to Florida but no one has visited Utah.

3. Ashley has cousins in Ohio Texas and Maine.

4. Ashley's cousin from Maine asked her to visit so she went there last summer.

Next Step: Write a sentence about three places you'd like to visit someday.

ELPS 2C, 4C

Use a Comma

Between a City and a State

El Paso, Texas

Between the Day and the Year

January 28, 2011

After the Greeting and Closing in a Letter

Dear Grandpa,   Love,
                        Liz

After Introductory Words

When we race, J. J. likes to win.

To Name a Person Spoken to

Annie, wait for me!

Commas 2
- **Commas in Dates and Addresses**
- **Commas in Letter Writing**

Copy the friendly letter below. Add commas where they are needed.

Example: February 2 2011

> February 2, 2011

254 Red Street
Lawton MI 49065
January 27 2011

Dear Groundhog

    Please cover your eyes when you come out of your burrow this year. I am tired of winter.

Sincerely
Bruce Limm

Next Step: Write a sentence using today's date.

TEKS 2.22C(ii)
ELPS 2C, 4C, 5E

Use an Apostrophe

To Make a Contraction

Two Words	Contraction
do not	don't
has not	hasn't
can not	can't
she is	she's
it is	it's
I am	I'm
we will	we'll
they will	they'll
is not	isn't
will not	won't
we are	we're
they are	they're

Apostrophes 1
● **Apostrophes to Make Contractions**

The two underlined words in each sentence can be made into a contraction. Write the contraction.

Example: We will go to the library.

We'll

1. We do not have to pay for books at the library.

2. It is a place where we can borrow them.

3. I am allowed to borrow books with my library card.

4. My sister Emma can not have her own library card.

5. She is just a baby!

Learning Language: Use a contraction in a sentence about your school library. Share your sentence with a partner.

TEKS 2.22C(iii)
ELPS 5E

Use an Apostrophe

To Show Ownership

This is Mary's book

The tree's leaves are falling.

My brother's frogs jump and croak.
(One brother owns the frogs.)

My brothers' frogs jump and croak.
(More than one brother owns the frogs.)

Apostrophes 2

- **Apostrophes to Show Ownership**

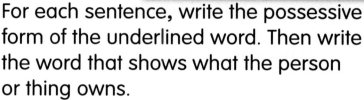

For each sentence, write the possessive form of the underlined word. Then write the word that shows what the person or thing owns.

Example: The <u>bird</u> eggs are colorful.

> bird's eggs

1. <u>Mom</u> ring is shiny.

2. I want to read <u>Mr. Green</u> book.

3. We found the <u>girl</u> backpack.

4. Do you know where <u>Becky</u> glasses are?

5. The <u>van</u> tire is flat.

Next Step: Write a sentence about something that belongs to your teacher. Use an apostrophe to show ownership.

ELPS 2C, 4C

Use Underlining

For Titles of Books and Magazines

I read <u>The Mouse That Snored</u>.

<u>Ranger Rick</u> comes in the mail.

Use Quotation Marks

Before and After a Speaker's Words

"I love carrots," said Sam.

 **Underlining and Quotation Marks**

Copy each sentence. Put quotation marks around a speaker's words. Underline any titles of books or magazines.

Example: Hi, Jared, said my dad.

> "Hi, Jared," said my dad.

1. When are you coming home? I asked.

2. He said, I'll be home soon.

3. My dad brought me a book called Lisa's Airplane Trip.

4. Thanks, Dad, I said.

5. I read the magazine Zoobooks every month.

Next Step: Write a sentence that tells the title of a book.

Using Other Rules for
Writing

In this section, you will learn other rules that will help you check the mechanics in your writing. You will learn the rules for using capital letters. You will learn the rules for making words plural. You will also learn how to use abbreviations. Following these rules helps readers understand what you write.

Use Capital Letters

For All Proper Nouns

Names, Titles, and Initials

➤ Jackie Wilson

Dr. Small

E. B. White

Days, Months, and Holidays

➤ Friday   January   Thanksgiving

Names of Places

➤ Canada   Rocky Mountains

Ohio   Main Street

Chicago   Sears Tower

practice

Capitalization 1
● **Proper Nouns**

Write all the words that should be capitalized in the sentences below. The number in ( ) tells how many words you should find in each sentence.

Example: We live on oak road in vicksburg. *(3)*

> Oak Road, Vicksburg

1. Mom and I wanted to surprise Dad for father's day. *(2)*

2. We asked Dad's old friend to meet us on sunday, june 14, in austin, texas. *(4)*

3. Dad and mr. hanks grew up in austin. *(3)*

4. Now Dad lives in dallas, and mr. hanks lives in houston. *(4)*

Next Step: Write today's date and your address.

Use Capital Letters

For the First Word in a Sentence
➜ Fireflies light up the garden.

For a Speaker's First Word
Mr. Smith said, "Look at this spiderweb."

For the Word "I"
What will I say to him?

For Titles of Books, Stories, Poems . . .
➜ Aesop's Fox (book)
"Lost in the Woods" (story)
"Elephant for Sale" (poem)
Spider (magazine)

practice

Capitalization 2 ?
- First Words
- The Word "I"
- Titles

For each sentence, write the word or words that should be capitalized.

Example: my neighbor couldn't figure it out.

<u>My</u>

1. Mr. Mark said, "this shelf should fit right here!"

2. he measured the space again.

3. then he looked in a book called <u>wood works</u>.

4. Mr. Mark also looked at a magazine article called "building shelves."

5. he looked at the pictures.

6. He said, "i made a mistake!"

Next Step: What do you think Mr. Mark did wrong? Write a sentence telling about it.

Make Plurals

Add -s to make the plural of most nouns.

    boy → boy**s**   wing → wing**s**

    shoe → shoe**s**   book → book**s**

Add -es to make the plural of nouns ending in *s, x, sh, ch,* and *z.*

    glass → glass**es**   inch → inch**es**

    fox → fox**es**   buzz → buzz**es**

    bush → bush**es**

TEKS 2.21A(ii)
ELPS 2C, 2G, 2H, 2I, 3E, 4C

Grammar practice

Plurals 1

- Most Nouns
- Nouns Ending in *s*, *x*, *sh*, *ch*, and *z*

Add **-s** or **-es** to each word to form the correct plural.

Example: pencil

pencils

---

1. rash

2. mess

3. flower

4. box

5. paper

6. wax

7. lunch

Learning Language: Choose one of the plurals you wrote. Write a sentence using the word. Then choose another word from the list above. Say a sentence to a partner using its plural form.

Make Plurals

Change the word to make the plural of some nouns. These are called "irregular" plurals.

| child → children | man → men |
| foot → feet | goose → geese |

Change the _y_ to _i_ and add _-es_ to nouns that end with a consonant plus _y_.

| sky → skies | story → stories |
| ferry → ferries | baby → babies |

TEKS 2.21A(ii)
ELPS 2C, 2G, 2H, 2I, 3E, 4C

Grammar Practice

Plurals 2
- Nouns Ending in a Consonant + y
- Irregular Plurals

Look at the rules on page 475. Then write the correct plural form for each word below.

Example: berry

berries

1. woman
2. penny
3. tooth
4. bunny
5. fly
6. mouse
7. daisy

Learning Language: Choose one of the plurals you wrote. Write a sentence using the word. Then choose another word from the list above. Say a sentence to a partner using its plural form.

Use Abbreviations

For Titles of People

Mister → Mr.   Doctor → Dr.

For Days of the Week

Sunday	Sun.	Thursday	Thurs.
Monday	Mon.	Friday	Fri.
Tuesday	Tues.	Saturday	Sat.
Wednesday	Wed.		

For Months of the Year

January	Jan.	July	July
February	Feb.	August	Aug.
March	Mar.	September	Sept.
April	Apr.	October	Oct.
May	May	November	Nov.
June	June	December	Dec.

Post Office Address Abbreviations

Avenue	AVE	Road	RD
Drive	DR	South	S
East	E	Street	ST
North	N	West	W

Abbreviations

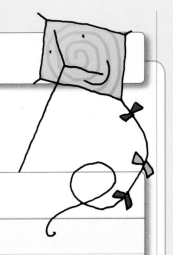

Write the abbreviation for each underlined word.

Example: <u>March</u> winds

> **Mar.**

1. 123 OAK <u>AVENUE</u>

2. Friday, <u>August</u> 29

3. 555 STATE <u>ROAD</u>

4. <u>January</u> 3

5. 869 <u>SOUTH</u> MAIN STREET

6. Thursday, <u>September</u> 18

Next Step: Write the correct abbreviations for all the days of the week.

Checking
Your Spelling

The spelling list that follows on pages 480–486 is in ABC order. It includes many of the important words you will use in your writing. Check this list when you are not sure how to spell a word. (Also check a classroom dictionary for help.)

Use a Spelling Plan

1. **Look** at the word and say it.
2. **Spell** it aloud.
3. **Say** the word again, sound by sound.
4. **Notice** the spelling of each sound.
5. **Cover** the word and write it on paper.
6. **Check** the spelling.
7. If it is wrong, **repeat** the plan.

ELPS 2C, 4C

A

about
after
again
all
alone
and
animal
another
are
as
ask
aunt
away

B

back
bad
bank
be
because
been

before
bell
best
big
black
blue
boat
book
born
both
box
bright
bring
broke
brother
brown
burn
but
by

C

call
candle
card
children
clean
clock
color
come
could
cousin
crowd

D

daddy
dance
dark
dear
didn't
doesn't
dogs
doll
dollars
done
don't
door
dream
drop

practice  Spelling 1

Look at the picture in front of each phrase below. Write a word from your spelling list to fill in the blank.

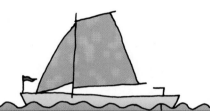

Example: sails on a _____

> **boat**

1. a _____ circle

2. a ringing _____

3. an open _____

4. $ a few _____

5. make a telephone _____

6. a _____ of water

Next Step: Write a sentence using one of the phrases above.

ELPS 2C, 4C

E

each
eat
eight
end
eye

F

fall
far
fast
feather
feel
fight
fire
first
five
floor
flowers
fly
food
foot

for
forgot
found
four
Friday
friend
from
front
full
fun
funny

G

game
girl
give
going
good
grandfather
grandmother
grass
green

H

had
hair
half
hand
happen
hard
has
have
head
help
her
here
hide
high
hill
his
home
hope
horse
hot
hour
how
hurt

I

I
ice
if
I'm
is
it's
I've

J

jam
jelly
just

K

keep
kids
kind
kitten
knew

practice Spelling 2

Write the correct word from your
spelling list to fill in the blank
in each sentence below.

Example: A baby cat is called a _____.

kitten

1. The day after Thursday is _____.

2. A joke is a _____ story.

3. Frozen water is _____.

4. There are 60 minutes in an _____.

5. I raise my _____ when I want to
speak in class.

Next Step: Write a sentence using another word from
your spelling list.

L

lady
land
last
laugh
leave
left
letter
light
live
long
look
lot
loud
love

M

made
make
many
may
men
milk

Monday
money
monkey
month
moon
more
morning
most
mother
move
much
must
my

N

name
need
new
next
nice
night
nine
not
now

O

of
off
okay
old
once
one
open
or
orange
other
our
out

P

party
pencil
penny
play
please
poor
porch
post

pour
pretty
pull
purple

Q

quick
quiet
quit

R

rabbit
rain
read
ready
really
ride
right
road
rode
room
rope

Spelling 3

Write a word from your spelling list to fill in the blanks in each sentence below. Pay attention to the hints.

Example: A r __ b __ __ __ has long ears.

rabbit

1. The sun does not shine at n __ __ h __ .

2. It rises every m __ __ n __ __ __ .

3. You may have an apple if you say
   p l __ __ __ __ .

4. Kris ate a juicy o __ __ __ __ __ .

5. My favorite color is p __ __ p __ __ .

Next Step: Write a sentence using another word from your spelling list.

ELPS 2C, 4C

S

said
Saturday
saw
say
says
school
seven
shoes
should
sister
six
sleep
soft
something
soon
sound
still
store
storm
street
summer
Sunday
sure

T

take
talk
teacher
teeth
tell
ten
thank
that
them
these
they
think
this
those
three
Thursday
told
tooth
try
Tuesday
two

U

uncle
under
until
use

V

van
very

W

walk
want
way
Wednesday
week
went
were
what
when
where

which
why
with
won
word
work
would
write

X

X-ray

Y

year
yellow
you
your
you're

Z

zipper
zoo

 **Spelling 4**

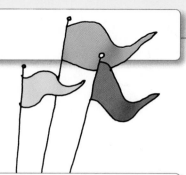

Write the correct word from your spelling list to answer each question below.

> Example: How many flags are in the picture?
>
> _three_

1. How many days are in a week?

2. Where do you go to see lions, monkeys, and bears?

3. What are the hard white things in your mouth?

4. What day comes after Tuesday?

5. What season is the hottest?

Next Step: Write a sentence using another word from your spelling list.

Using the
Right Word

Some words sound alike, but they have different spellings. They also have different meanings. These words are called **homophones**.

| ant | Mom bought me an ant farm. |
| aunt | My aunt is my dad's sister. |

| ate | I ate a banana this morning. |
| eight | Shannon is eight years old. |

| bare | Look at my bare feet! |
| bear | The grizzly bear growled. |

blew
blue

Dakota blew the biggest bubble.

A robin's egg is blue.

by
buy

Place the spoon by the knife.

We must buy some milk today.

dear
deer

My grandma is a dear woman.

The deer ran into the woods.

for
four

Miss Nelson made lunch for us.

Nick ate four tacos.

ELPS 1C, 1E, 2C, 2G, 2H, 2I, 3B, 3E, 4C, 5B

practice

Using the Right Word 1

- blew, blue
- buy, by
- dear, deer
- for, four

For each sentence, write the correct word from the choice given.

Example: Jimmy *(blew, blue)* into the whistle toy.

blew

---

1. It was his *(dear, deer)* grandma's birthday!

2. She told Jim not to *(buy, by)* a gift.

3. He made a painting *(for, four)* her.

4. He used a lot of *(blew, blue)* paint.

5. He painted a *(dear, deer)* with antlers.

6. He painted *(for, four)* kinds of flowers, too.

Learning Language: Write a sentence telling about a picture you would like to paint. Use the word *by* in your sentence. Then tell a partner about the picture using the word *buy*.

hear
here

I like to hear birds sing.

Who sits here?

its
it's

The dog ate its food.

I think it's about 8:00.

(it's = it is)

knew
new

I knew my ABC's last year.

We have a new girl in our class.

know
no

Do you know her name?

Robert said, "No, I don't."

ELPS 1C, 1E, 2C, 2G, 2H, 2I, 3B, 3E, 4C, 5B

practice

Using the Right Word 2

- hear, here
- its, it's
- knew, new
- know, no

Write the correct word for each sentence.

Example: I have a *(knew, new)* joke to tell you.

**new**

1. Maxine, are you ready to *(hear, here)* it?

2. *(Its, It's)* about bees going to school.

3. Do you *(know, no)* how they get there?

4. Maxine said, "*(Know, No)*, tell me."

5. A bee gets to school on *(its, it's)* buzz.

6. She laughed and said, "I *(knew, new)* it would be a funny one!"

Learning Language: Write a sentence telling how you get to school. Use one of the blue words at the top of the page in your sentence. Then tell a partner a sentence using the homophone of the word you chose.

| one | My baby brother is one year old. |
| won | Liz won a prize at the fair. |

	We used their bikes.
their	(Their shows ownership.)
there	There are four of them.
they're	They're mountain bikes.
	(they're = they are)

to	I like to read funny books.
two	I read two joke books today.
too	Joe likes joke books, too.

ELPS 1C, 1E, 2C, 2G, 2H, 2I, 3B, 3E, 4C, 5B

practice

Using the Right Word 3
- one, won
- their, there, they're
- to, two, too

Write the correct word for each sentence.

Example: Mom *(one, won)* a fruit basket as a prize at the school carnival.

won

1. The basket had *(one, won)* apple in it.

2. It had bananas, *(to, too, two)*.

3. *(Their, There, They're)* were some cherries, too.

4. Mom is going *(to, too, two)* make a fruit salad.

5. Dad will eat *(to, too, two)* bowls of fruit.

Learning Language: Write a sentence about winning a prize. Use the word *their* in your sentence. Then tell about winning the prize to a partner using the words *there* and *they're*.

Antonyms

Antonyms are two words with opposite meanings. Here are some common antonyms you should know.

above	—	below
clean	—	dirty
day	—	night
fast	—	slow
first	—	last
happy	—	sad
hard	—	soft
high	—	low
hot	—	cold
laugh	—	cry
left	—	right
loud	—	quiet
on	—	off
push	—	pull
short	—	tall
up	—	down
win	—	lose

ELPS 1C, 1E, 2C, 2G, 2H, 2I, 3B, 3E

practice | Antonyms

Finish each sentence below with the opposite (antonym) of the word under the line.

Example: Matthew's house is on the _____ side of the street.
(left)

right

---

1. Yesterday it was _____ outside.
   (cold)

2. The teacher asked the children to be _____ .
   (loud)

3. It's too bad we did not _____ this game.
   (lose)

4. Someone left the light _____ .
   (off)

5. I like my pillow. It is not too _____ .
   (hard)

Learning Language: Write a sentence like those above. Use any pair of antonyms that was not used here. Then tell a partner a sentence using the antonym of *down*.

Understanding
Sentences

A **sentence** tells a complete idea and has two parts.

> 1. The **subject** is the naming part.
> 2. The **predicate** (verb) is the telling part.

The verb tells what the subject is doing.

My <u>mom</u> <u>rides</u> a motorcycle.
     subject verb

A **sentence** begins with a capital letter. It ends with a period, a question mark, or an exclamation point.

Grandpa climbs trees.
Can he reach the top?
Wow, he is way up there!

ELPS 2C, 4C

The Subject

The **subject** is the naming part of a sentence. It tells who or what the sentence is about. A subject is usually a noun that names a person, place, or thing.

My new baby sister sleeps a lot.

(*Sister* is the main word in the subject. It is the simple subject.)

My new baby sister **sleeps a lot.**

(*My new baby sister* is the complete subject. The complete subject includes the main word along with any other words that describe it.)

The subject can also be a pronoun.

She **went to the mall.**

It **is a new car.**

We **will listen to music.**

ELPS 2C, 2G, 2H, 2I, 3E, 4C

Subject of a Sentence

For each sentence, write the complete subject.

Example: The explorer read his treasure map.

The explorer

1. The explorer's shirt was striped.
2. He wore a dark blue hat.
3. His old, torn map led to a chest.
4. A dotted line showed the way.
5. The chest could hold gold.
6. It could hold a very old book or a vase.

Learning Language: Write a sentence about what kind of buried treasure the explorer found. Underline the complete subject. Then tell a partner what the explorer did with the treasure. Identify the complete subject of your sentence.

The Predicate

The **predicate** is the telling part of a sentence. It contains the **verb**. The predicate either tells what the subject is doing, or it tells something about the subject.

My uncle Benny builds doghouses.

(*Builds* is the verb in the predicate.)

My uncle Benny builds doghouses.

(*Builds doghouses* is the complete predicate.)

That flower is beautiful.

(The verb *is* and the word *beautiful* form the complete predicate. This predicate tells something about the subject.)

ELPS 2C, 4C

Grammar practice: Predicate of a Sentence

For each sentence, write the complete predicate.

Example: The stoplight turned red.

turned red

---

1. Mom stopped the car.

2. Two kids pressed the *walk* button.

3. They crossed the street.

4. They were very careful.

5. The light changed to green.

6. They went on their way.

Learning Language: Write a sentence about a car trip. Underline the complete predicate. Then tell a partner where you would go on a car trip. Identify the complete predicate of your sentence.

TEKS 2.21C
ELPS 2C, 3C, 4C

Kinds of Sentences

A **telling sentence** makes a statement.

Soccer is my favorite game.

An **asking sentence** asks a question.

Will you play with me?

A **command sentence** makes a request or gives directions.

Kick with the side of your foot.

An **exclamatory sentence** shows surprise or strong feelings.

Watch out for the ball!

Kinds of Sentences

Write a letter for each sentence.
Write **T** for telling, **A** for asking,
E for exclamatory, and **C** for command.

Example: How do birds stay dry when it rains?

A

1. Feathers protect a bird from getting too wet.

2. Wow, some birds cannot fly!

3. Do you have a pet bird at home?

4. Clean its cage often.

5. My aunt has a myna bird.

6. Can a myna "talk" better than a parrot?

Learning Language: Write a sentence about a bird. Ask a classmate to tell what kind of sentence you have written. Then say a sentence about a bird. Ask a classmate to tell what kind of sentence you said.

Using the
Parts of Speech

All of the words you use fit into eight groups. These groups are called the **parts of speech**.

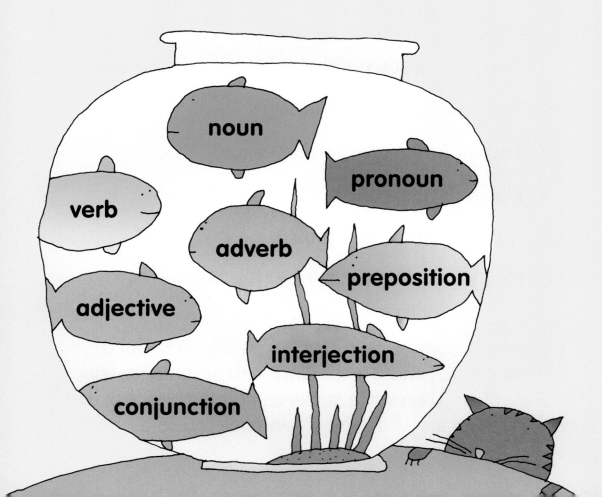

Nouns

A **noun** is a word that names a person, place, or thing.

person: girl   firefighter
place: house   school
thing: bike   flower

Nouns can be **common** or **proper**.

common: boy   street
proper: Gus   Oak Street

TEKS 2.21A(ii), 2.22B(i)
ELPS 2C, 2G, 2H, 2I, 3E, 4C

Nouns 1
● Common and Proper Nouns

Write the nouns you find in each sentence. (The number of nouns in each sentence is given at the end of the sentence.) Underline the proper nouns.

Example: Tito and his family are planning a trip. *(3)*

> <u>Tito</u>, family, trip

---

1. Tito wants to swim in the Pacific Ocean. *(2)*

2. Val would like to see the Rocky Mountains. *(2)*

3. Ricky likes beaches. *(2)*

4. Their dad likes campgrounds in Vermont. *(3)*

Learning Language: Write a sentence about a trip you would like to take. Ask a classmate to underline each noun in your sentence. Then tell two sentences about a trip you have been on. Ask a classmate to identify the nouns that you say.

Nouns

Nouns can be **singular** or **plural**.

singular: neighbor house

plural: neighbors houses

A **possessive noun** shows ownership.
Add **'s** after a singular noun.

Julie's flute

the bird's wings

Add only an apostrophe (') after most plural nouns.

The boys' camp is near the lake.

There were eggs in both birds' nests.

Grammar Practice

Nouns 2
- Singular and Plural Nouns
- Possessive Nouns

Make two columns. Write the singular nouns from the paragraph below in one column. Write the plural nouns in the other column.

Example: Pamela watered the plants.

Singular	Plural
Pamela	plants

Hank likes Mr. Green's garden. Mr. Green asked Hank and Pamela to help him. They dug a little hole for each seed. They planted tomatoes and potatoes. They also planted beans, peas, carrots, and onions. When they harvest their crops, they will have a big meal.

Learning Language: Read the paragraph again. Write down the possessive noun that you find. Then use singular and plural nouns to tell a partner what you would plant in a garden.

Pronouns

A **pronoun** is a word that takes the place of a noun. Here are some pronouns.

singular:

I	my	your	her	him	it
me	you	she	he	his	its

plural:

we	you	our	them
us	your	they	their

Pronouns stand for nouns in sentences.

(*She* stands for *Holly*.)

Holly **played a game.**
She **hid the penny.**

(*He* stands for *Erik*. *It* stands for *kite*.)

Erik **made a** kite.
Then he **flew** it.

TEKS 2.21A(vi)
ELPS 2C, 2G, 2H, 2I, 3E, 4C, 5E

Grammar practice — Pronouns

For each sentence below, write the pronoun. Then write the noun it stands for.

Example: The bird broke its wing.

> its — bird

1. Rena braids her long hair.

2. Davon, you may have a snack.

3. Mom made dinner, and the family enjoyed it.

4. Ted said, "My backpack is heavy."

5. Luke and Kenny raised their hands at the same time.

6. The teacher saw Luke first and picked him.

Learning Language: Write one or two sentences about a friend. Use a pronoun to take the place of a noun. Then use a pronoun to tell why you are a good friend.

Verbs

A **verb** is a word that shows action or helps complete a thought (linking verb).

> **Spot barks at my neighbor.** (action verb)
>
> **Mr. Wilson is so mad!** (linking verb)

Common Linking Verbs:

is	are	was	been
were	am	be	

Some Action Verbs:

ask	fix	jump	play
cook	help	listen	ride
dance	hug	move	stop

512

Grammar practice

Verbs 1
● Action and Linking Verbs

Write the verb in each sentence below. Then write **A** for action or **L** for linking.

Example: Katy listens to her CD.

> listens, A

1. She owns a CD player.

2. Katy likes country music.

3. Her favorite song is "Country Mile."

4. Sometimes she dances to the music.

5. She is a good dancer.

6. Katy also sings well.

Learning Language: Write one or two sentences about the kind of music you like. Underline the verb or verbs. Then tell why you like that kind of music using one action verb and one linking verb.

Verb Tenses

Some verbs tell what is happening now, or in the **present**.

Sarah walks her dog every morning.

Some verbs tell what happened in the **past**.

Sarah walked her dog last night.

(Many verbs in our language are **regular**. This means you add *-ed* to form the past tense.)

Some verbs tell what will happen in the **future**.

Sarah will walk her dog tomorrow.

 **TEKS** 2.21A(i)
ELPS 2C, 2G, 2H, 2I, 3E, 4C, 5E

Grammar practice

Verbs 2
● **Verb Tenses**

Write the action verb in each sentence below. Then write **present, past,** or **future**.

Example: I save money in my piggy bank.

save, present

---

1. Tina saved more than six dollars last month.

2. She puts all her change in a pretty box.

3. Jane will buy a new baseball glove.

4. Her brother tossed the ball to Jane.

5. She wants a catcher's mitt.

Learning Language: Write a sentence about saving money using the past, present, and future tenses. Then use all three tenses to tell about why saving money is important.

Irregular Verbs

Some verbs are **irregular**. You usually can't add **-ed** to them. They change in different ways.

Present Tense	Past Tense	With Helping Verb
am, is, are	was, were	been
begin	began	begun
break	broke	broken
catch	caught	caught
come	came	come
draw	drew	drawn
eat	ate	eaten
fall	fell	fallen
give	gave	given
go	went	gone
hide	hid	hidden, hid
know	knew	known
ride	rode	ridden
run	ran	run
see	saw	seen
sing	sang, sung	sung
take	took	taken
throw	threw	thrown
write	wrote	written

Grammar practice

Verbs 3
● Irregular Verbs

TEKS 2.21A(i)
ELPS 2C, 2G, 2H, 2I, 3E, 4C, 5E

Read each sentence below. Complete each with the past tense of the verb in parentheses. (Look on page 515 for help.)

Example: A friendly cat _____ to our door. *(come)*

came

1. We _____ her some milk and food. *(give)*

2. The cat _____ it all up. *(eat)*

3. Then she _____ our dog. *(see)*

4. The cat quickly _____ into the bushes. *(run)*

5. She _____ there for a long time. *(hide)*

Learning Language: Write a sentence about an animal. Use the past tense form of an irregular verb. Then tell a partner another sentence about the animal using the past tense form of a different irregular verb.

Adjectives

An **adjective** is a word that describes a noun or pronoun.

> **Large** snakes live in the jungle.
>
> An **anaconda** is a **giant** one!

The words *a, an,* and *the* are **articles**. Use *a* before a consonant sound:

> **a parrot**

Use *an* before a vowel sound:

> **an otter**

Adjectives 1
● Adjectives and Articles

Write the adjectives and articles from each sentence below. The number in ( ) tells you how many you will find.

Example: The old airplane flew in circles. (2)

The, old

1. The plane made loud noises. (2)

2. It left long trails of white smoke. (2)

3. The smoke looked like huge letters. (2)

4. The little plane was writing! (2)

5. The blue sky had a funny message. (4)

Learning Language: Write a sentence that tells what the plane wrote. Use adjectives and articles. Then tell a partner why the plane wrote what it did using adjectives and articles.

TEKS 2.21A(iii)
ELPS 2C, 2G, 2H, 2I, 3B, 3E, 4C

Adjectives That Compare

An **adjective** sometimes compares two nouns (or pronouns).

> An ant is smaller than an anaconda.
>
> A lion's roar is louder than a cat's meow.

An **adjective** can also compare more than two nouns.

> The anteater is the oddest animal in our zoo.
>
> The biggest mammal in the world is the whale.

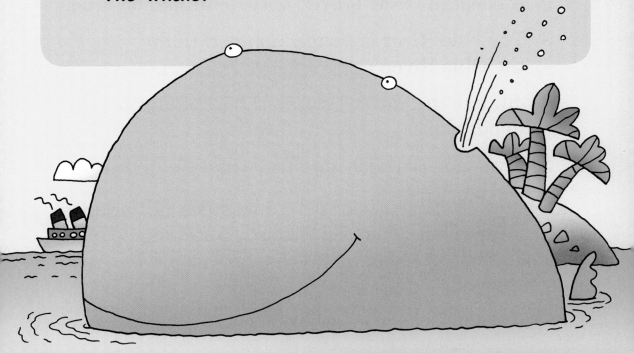

Grammar practice

Adjectives 2
● **Adjectives That Compare**

For each sentence, write the correct adjective.

> Example: An elephant is *(bigger, biggest)* than a hippo.
>
> bigger

1. The *(hotter, hottest)* place in the United States is Death Valley.

2. A cheetah is the *(faster, fastest)* animal on land.

3. The Nile River is *(longer, longest)* than the Ohio River.

4. Jill has the *(darker, darkest)* hair of anyone in our class.

5. My dog is *(smaller, smallest)* than Ken's dog.

Learning Language: Write a sentence that includes an adjective that compares. Then say a sentence to a partner using an adjective to compare two activities you enjoy doing.

Adverbs

An **adverb** is a word that describes a verb.
It can tell *how, where,* or *when.*

How: Erin ran quickly.

Where: She fell down.

When: She has fallen before.

Here are some other adverbs.

How: brightly   carefully   easily

fast   loudly   quietly

Where: away   forward   nearby

outside   there   upstairs

When: always   first   often

weekly   yearly   yesterday

TEKS 2.21A(iv)
ELPS 2C, 2G, 2H, 2I, 3E, 4C

Grammar practice  Adverbs

Write the adverb you find in each sentence below. Hint: Look for the action verb first.

Example: The fish swam away.

away

1. Teddy quietly read his book.

2. We went swimming yesterday.

3. Mom slowly added milk to the gravy.

4. Sunflowers grow fast.

5. Donna walks there.

6. The airplane glided smoothly to a stop.

Learning Language: Write a sentence that uses an adverb. Then say a sentence with an adverb.

Prepositions, Conjunctions, and Interjections

A **preposition** is used to help make a statement.

> Maya laughed at the joke.
>
> Joe sat on the beach.

A **conjunction** connects words or ideas.

> I will dance or sing.
>
> First I cried, and then I laughed.

An **interjection** shows excitement.

> Wow! Did you see that bug?
>
> Yuck! I hate creepy crawlers!

TEKS 2.21A(v)
ELPS 2C, 2G, 2H, 2I, 3C, 3E, 4C, 5F

Grammar practice

Prepositions, Conjunctions, and Interjections

Write the correct word to complete each sentence.

> Example: *(Wow, Oh no)*, Isabel is a good cheerleader!
>
> _Wow_

Prepositions

1. Jake ran *(up, in)* the stairs.

Conjunctions

2. I can choose a pear *(or, but)* an apple.

Interjections

3. Marvin scared me when he said, "*(Boo, Gosh)*!"

Learning Language: Write three sentences. Use at least one preposition, one conjunction, and one interjection. Then say three sentences using the same three parts of speech.

Prepositional Phrases

A **prepositional phrase** is a preposition and the noun or pronoun following it.

The picture hangs on **the wall.**

The cats sleep under **the bed.**

TEKS 2.21A(v)
ELPS 2C, 2G, 2H, 2I, 3E, 4C

Grammar practice

Prepositional Phrases

Write the prepositional phrases in the following sentences.

Example: I put an apple on my lunch tray.

> on my lunch tray

1. I slipped on a banana peel.

2. The puppies hid behind their mother.

3. Jorge stood on the ladder.

4. Jodie kicked the soccer ball across the street.

5. The puzzle pieces are inside the box.

6. At the circus, we saw clowns and lions.

Learning Language: Write a question with a prepositional phrase and read it to a partner. Your partner should answer using a prepositional phrase. Then switch roles.

Credits

Text:
English Language Proficiency Standards and Texas Essential Knowledge and Skills Copyright © Texas Education Agency

P. 269: Copyright © 2003 by Houghton Mifflin Harcourt Publishing Company. Adapted and reproduced by permission from *The American Heritage First Dictionary.*

Photo:
P. 282 (tl) ©Rolf Nussbaumer/Alamy; **282** (tr) ©Ingram Publishing/Getty Images; **282** (cl) ©Tom Uhlman/Alamy; **282** (cr) ©Tim Davis/Corbis; **282** (bl) ©Jupiter; **282** (br), **285** (b), **358** ©Corbis; **284** ©Comstock/Getty Images; **285** (t) ©Photodisc/Getty Images; **285** (c) ©Hemera Technologies/Jupiter Images; **340** ©Image Source/Getty Images; **346** ©Morgan Lane Photography/Alamy; **352** Harcourt Photo Studio; **364** ©Andersen Ross/Blend Images/Getty Images; **370** ©Richard Lewisohn/Digital Vision/Getty Images; **376** ©JUPITERIMAGES/Bananastock/Alamy.

Texas Essential Knowledge and Skills (TEKS) for English Language Arts

The TEKS are the skills you need to master by the end of Grade 2. The first column in the chart below lists the English Language Arts TEKS. The second column shows where these TEKS are taught in *Texas Write Source*.

⭐ TEKS 2.17 Writing/Writing Process

Students use elements of the writing process (planning, drafting, revising, editing, and publishing) to compose text. Students are expected to:

A plan a first draft by generating ideas for writing (e.g., drawing, sharing ideas, listing key ideas);	pages 7, 23, 26, 42, 47, 49, 54, 55, 59, 62, 63, 92, 93, 98, 99, 106, 136, 137, 142–144, 152, 153, 178, 179, 184, 190, 191, 202, 203, 212, 213, 218, 219, 222, 223, 228–231, 244–247, 260–262, 290–293, 428, 429, 432
B develop drafts by sequencing ideas through writing sentences;	pages 8, 22, 26, 43, 47, 49, 56, 59, 61, 64–69, 100, 104, 105, 110, 111, 137, 145, 154, 155, 179, 185, 192–195, 204, 205, 214, 220, 223, 232–237, 248–253, 296–301, 420–424, 434, 440
C revise drafts by adding or deleting words, phrases, or sentences;	pages 10, 11, 26, 44, 47, 57, 70, 71, 74–77, 101, 114–121, 146, 156, 157, 160–163, 186, 193, 196, 206, 214, 238, 254, 264, 302–309, 314, 320
D edit drafts for grammar, punctuation, and spelling using a teacher-developed rubric; and	pages 12, 26, 30, 31, 82, 83, 126, 127, 168, 169

*Page References in *Student Edition*
*Page References in *SkillsBook*

E publish and share writing with others.

pages 14, 15, 17–19, 32–35, 37, 47, 49, 57, 84, 101, 128, 170–172, 198, 208, 215, 221, 240, 256, 257, 266, 314–316, 321, 326

⬚ TEKS 2.18 Writing/Literary Texts

Students write literary texts to express their ideas and feelings about real or imagined people, events, and ideas. Students are expected to:

A write brief stories that include a beginning, middle, and end; and

pages 22, 60, 61, 64–77, 80–83, 88, 89, 232–237

B write short poems that convey sensory details.

pages 261–264, 267, 268, 437

⬚ TEKS 2.19 Writing/Expository and Procedural Texts

Students write expository and procedural or work-related texts to communicate ideas and information to specific audiences for specific purposes. Students are expected to:

A write brief compositions about topics of interest to the student;

pages 46, 47, 92, 93, 96–101, 130, 131, 136, 137, 286–309, 312–315

B write short letters that put ideas in a chronological or logical sequence and use appropriate conventions (e.g., date, salutation, closing); and

pages 48, 49, 86, 87, 90, 91, 102–105, 107–121, 124–128, 132–135, 149–151, 154, 155, 158, 159, 166–169, 176, 177, 440–442

C write brief comments on literary or informational texts.

pages 129, 173, 184, 190, 191, 199, 202, 203, 209, 213, 219, 222, 223

⬚ TEKS 2.20 Writing/Persuasive Texts

pages 140–163, 166–171, 174–179

Students write persuasive texts to influence the attitudes or actions of a specific audience on specific issues. Students are expected to write persuasive statements about issues that are important to the student for the appropriate audience in the school, home, or local community.

*Page References in *Student Edition*
*Page References in *SkillsBook*

530

Students understand the function of and use the conventions of academic language when speaking and writing. Students continue to apply earlier standards with greater complexity. Students are expected to:

A understand and use the following parts of speech in the context of reading, writing, and speaking: (i) verbs (past, present, and future); (ii) nouns (singular/plural, common/proper); (iii) adjectives (e.g., descriptive: old, wonderful; articles: a, an, the); (iv) adverbs (e.g., time: before, next; manner: carefully, beautifully); (v) prepositions and prepositional phrases; (vi) pronouns (e.g., he, him); and (vii) time-order transition words;	pages 22, 25, 45, 56, 57, 61, 78–83, 104, 105, 110, 111, 116, 117, 122–127, 147, 234, 239, 247, 255, 265, 305, 310–313, 385–389, 392–401, 404–409, 434, 447, 448, 473–476, 505–510, 513–526 pages 69–78, 119–124, 127–132, 137–159
B use complete sentences with correct subject-verb agreement; and	pages 164, 166–169, 187, 197, 207, 265, 402, 403, 416, 418, 419 pages 111, 112
C distinguish among declarative and interrogative sentences.	pages 47, 165, 168, 169, 197, 207, 239, 255, 265, 417, 502, 503 pages 107–110

Students write legibly and use appropriate capitalization and punctuation conventions in their compositions. Students are expected to:

B use capitalization for: (i) proper nouns; (ii) months and days of the week; and (iii) the salutation and closing of a letter; and	pages 25, 45, 80–83, 85–87, 90, 91, 124, 126, 127, 147, 166–169, 187, 197, 207, 239, 255, 265, 312, 313, 386, 469, 470, 505, 506 pages 45–56, 65–68
C recognize and use punctuation marks, including: (i) ending punctuation in sentences; (ii) apostrophes and contractions; and (iii) apostrophes and possessives.	pages 25, 45, 66, 67, 80–83, 124, 125, 147, 165–169, 187, 197, 207, 239, 255, 265, 312, 313, 390, 397, 454–457, 462–465, 507, 508 pages 3, 4, 7–14, 29–36, 125, 126

*Page References in *Student Edition*
*Page References in *SkillsBook*

⬚ TEKS 2.24 Research/Research Plan

Students ask open-ended research questions and develop a plan for answering them. Students are expected to:

A generate a list of topics of class-wide interest and formulate open-ended questions about one or two of the topics; and

pages 106, 131, 274, 290, 292–295, 428–430

B decide what sources of information might be relevant to answer these questions.

pages 274, 279, 291, 294, 295, 430

⬚ TEKS 2.25 Research/Gathering Sources

Students determine, locate, and explore the full range of relevant sources addressing a research question and systematically record the information they gather. Students are expected to:

A gather evidence from available sources (natural and personal) as well as from interviews with local experts;

pages 274, 277, 280, 292–295, 318, 319, 323, 430

B use text features (e.g., table of contents, alphabetized index, headings) in age-appropriate reference works (e.g., picture dictionaries) to locate information; and

pages 274, 282, 284, 285, 291, 293, 379–381

C record basic information in simple visual formats (e.g., notes, charts, picture graphs, diagrams).

pages 274, 292–295, 319, 323–325, 449, 450

⬚ TEKS 2.26 Research/Synthesizing Information

Students clarify research questions and evaluate and synthesize collected information. Students are expected to revise the topic as a result of answers to initial research questions.

pages 275, 293, 297–299, 302, 303

⬚ TEKS 2.27 Research/Organizing and Presenting Ideas

Students organize and present their ideas and information according to the purpose of the research and their audience. Students (with adult assistance) are expected to create a visual display or dramatization to convey the results of the research.

pages 32, 33, 275, 316, 318–326, 449, 450

English Language Proficiency Standards (ELPS)

The English Language Proficiency Standards (ELPS) outline expectations for students who are learning English. The first column in the chart below lists selected ELPS for English Language Arts. The second column shows where these ELPS are taught in *Texas Write Source*.

⭐ ELPS 3 Speaking

Cross-curricular second language acquisition/speaking. The ELL speaks in a variety of modes for a variety of purposes with an awareness of different language registers (formal/informal) using vocabulary with increasing fluency and accuracy in language arts and all content areas. ELLs may be at the beginning, intermediate, advanced, or advanced high stage of English language acquisition in speaking. In order for the ELL to meet grade-level learning expectations across the foundation and enrichment curriculum, all instruction delivered in English must be linguistically accommodated (communicated, sequenced, and scaffolded) commensurate with the student's level of English language proficiency. The student is expected to:

A	practice producing sounds of newly acquired vocabulary such as long and short vowels, silent letters, and consonant clusters to pronounce English words in a manner that is increasingly comprehensible	pages 327, 331, 343, 349, 479
G	express opinions, ideas, and feelings ranging from communicating single words and short phrases to participating in extended discussions on a variety of social and grade-appropriate academic topics	pages 2, 4, 15, 27, 33, 37, 151, 164, 194, 195, 228, 229, 259, 339, 341, 342, 344, 345, 347, 351, 353, 354, 357, 359, 360, 363, 365, 375, 377, 422
H	narrate, describe, and explain with increasing specificity and detail as more English is acquired	pages 327, 336, 338, 339, 341, 342, 344, 347, 348, 350, 353, 354, 357, 365, 369, 370, 371, 377

*Page References in *Student Edition*
*Page References in *SkillsBook*

⬚ ELPS **4** Reading

Cross-curricular second language acquisition/reading. The ELL reads a variety of texts for a variety of purposes with an increasing level of comprehension in all content areas. ELLs may be at the beginning, intermediate, advanced, or advanced high stage of English language acquisition in reading. In order for the ELL to meet grade-level learning expectations across the foundation and enrichment curriculum, all instruction delivered in English must be linguistically accommodated (communicated, sequenced, and scaffolded) commensurate with the student's level of English language proficiency. For kindergarten and first grade, certain of these student expectations apply to text read aloud for students not yet at the stage of decoding written text. The student is expected to:

C   develop basic sight vocabulary, derive meaning of environmental print, and comprehend English vocabulary and language structures used routinely in written classroom materials

⭐ ELPS 5 Writing

Cross-curricular second language acquisition/writing. The ELL writes in a variety of forms with increasing accuracy to effectively address a specific purpose and audience in all content areas. ELLs may be at the beginning, intermediate, advanced, or advanced high stage of English language acquisition in writing. In order for the ELL to meet grade-level learning expectations across foundation and enrichment curriculum, all instruction delivered in English must be linguistically accommodated (communicated, sequenced, and scaffolded) commensurate with the student's level of English language proficiency. For kindergarten and first grade, certain of these student expectations do not apply until the student has reached the stage of generating original written text using a standard writing system. The student is expected to:

B	write using newly acquired basic vocabulary and content-based grade-level vocabulary	pages 331, 335, 337, 338, 343, 349, 350, 355, 361, 362, 367, 368, 373, 445, 488–494
		pages 87–98
G	narrate, describe, and explain with increasing specificity and detail to fulfill content area writing needs as more English is acquired	pages 39, 41, 43, 47, 49, 51, 53, 56, 58, 59, 61, 64–69, 87, 89, 92, 93, 95–97, 100, 102, 103, 105, 108–113, 131, 133, 135–137, 155, 160–163, 175, 177–179, 186, 192, 194–196, 205, 206, 222, 233, 234, 238, 254, 264, 275, 297–307, 324, 433, 443, 444

Index

This index will help you find specific information in the handbook. Entries in italic are words from the "Using the Right Word" section. The colored boxes contain information you will use often.

542

traits of writing, *see* writing traits.